WHEN YOU ARE
BURSTING

PATRICK COMBS

WHEN YOU ARE BURSTING

Hilarious, Sad, Passionate Stories from
an Unusual Everyman

Published by: CYL Publications http://cylp.co

ISBN: 1-940324-19-X

ISBN-13: 978-1-940324-19-7

Contents

Introduction

You know those moments in your life that you look back on and see as life defining? 1992 in a small theatre in San Francisco watching monologist Spalding Gray sit behind a desk on stage and engross us all with the story of trying to finish his novel. The show was called Monster in a Box. That's the night this book was conceived. It just took twenty four years to birth it.

I left that night with a burning desire to entertain people with stories from my life. Way back then, I was too terrified to do it live on stage as Spald did so masterfully, but I am forever grateful that I quickly began writing my stories down. I had no idea how to write a good story so I bought Spalding's book of personal stories and studied his technique. Yet, story after story, I sucked at writing.

I was about two years and 10 stories deep into trying to learn the craft when something unexpected and wonderful happened. A $95,093.35 junk-mail check arrived at my home and ended up giving me one hell of a story to tell. The only problem was that it was an Everest of a story. It was a very long story with more writing demands than I had ever come close to facing. Before the check story, I was working with short stories from life.

Suddenly I was facing a mountain of story, but one that I knew had gold in it if only I could tell it well. I was completely frightened and intimidated by the gargantuan size of the junk-mail check story, but I threw myself into the task with total abandon.

For six day and six nights I took breaks only long enough to cram some food in my mouth or to sleep for four hours. I totally immersed myself into the writing from sun up to long past sun down. I agonized at the keyboard trying to tell the story well. I hit that glorious point of no return when the writer stops writing the story and the story starts writing itself. I was getting a crash course in being completely committed to the story and ambitiously facing the challenge of giving my all to the story, line after never ending line.

At the end of those six days and six nights of obsession, I was entirely exhausted and thoroughly wiped, but I had my first draft. And then I posted it online.

It absolutely exploded into an internet sensation. It might not be outrageous to say that in 1995 when I posted the story - that eventually became my book *MAN 1, BANK 0* - that it became the most popular personal story on the internet for a year or more. It achieved millions of reads and I got thousands upon thousands of emails. And the attention the junk-check story drew rubbed off onto the handful of other stories I had previously written, so I suddenly had readers. Readers gave me reason to keep writing.

That's the story of how I got my start on writing stories and I've been doing it since then.

Aside from the singular story, *MAN 1, BANK 0*, this is the first time I've put my personal stories into a book. I thought it was time. I felt like I finally had the right stories to do what I hope this book will do.

The day I first saw Spalding Gray tell a story from his life, what I fell in love with was a well told story's ability to help us lose ourselves in the moment, lighten our load with laughter or awe, and ultimately show us something good about ourselves. I hope stories in this book are able to do that for you.

I also tell my stories in hopes they will inspire you to tell yours. Writing your stories makes you fall deeper in love with life. Do it! Grab a pen and paper, or run to your computer and write a story from you life. Then send it to me. goodthinkpc@gmail.com. I'll be your first fan.

Here's what I've learned from writing out my stories. Stories bond us. Stories show us we have a lot in common. We're all the same on the inside, we're all in this thing called life together, and truly we're all human. We live, we love, we laugh, we cry, we screw up, we fall apart, we fail, we lose, we win, we get lost, we get found and we learn. And through all these experiences, every single one of them, life gifts us a beautiful story to share. These are my stories.

Patrick Combs
September 6, 2016
Encinitas, CA

Breakdown

Yesterday, I was having a parent breakdown. I was doing my best to not completely lose my #!@!. I just wanted the sound of my son's voice out of my head! I was suffering from a total loss of patience, and on the verge of being a complete A-hole to my child.

I don't know exactly why I lost my patience, but I was hanging onto friendliness by my fingernails.

My son Will is 7 years old. I would throw myself in front of a train for him without a moment's hesitation. He is everything wonderful and good in the world, and completely innocent in this story. But yesterday, I was insanely annoyed by his every utterance.

Recently, he hit a new phase in his development. I call it, "Never stop talking, ever, ever, Say everything I think, I talk therefore I am, When in doubt, say it. The best thing about life is talking, Silence is Death, Dad who do you think would win?"

For the past 4 days, it's been like being locked in a room with Robin Williams - while he's on LSD!

I'm hanging onto my sanity by a thread.

I usually love the sound of my son's voice. I'm usually present to his every question and conversation. I usually am calm, loving, and nice.

But I've been with my son, non-stop, morning to night for 96 hours. My wife's away in Cancun at a resort drinking Mai Tai's... Whatever... And my son's school hasn't been in session since Wednesday...

So say this with me slowly, "N-o-n s-t-o-p, R-e-l-e-n-t-l-e-s-s, H-e-l-p-M-e-!"

Seriously, imagine being locked in a room with Robin Williams while he's on LSD... Really, let that soak in.

And then please, immediately come over to my house, and club me unconscious.

These are exact quotes from my son yesterday in a single hour.

"Dad, Dad, what would you do if a friddle frog came into our front room?"

(Followed by chanting, "friddle frog frog frog frog frog frog frog frog" for what I believe to be a year and a half.)... [I have zero idea what a friddle frog is and nor do I care].

Followed by...

"Dad, Dad, look. Dad, look! DAD LOOK! Look at me throw the ball. Look at me touching the cat. Dad, look at the cat looking at the ball I threw!"

Then without pause or a breath...

"Dad, Dad, do you know what Swinter is? It's a combination between summer and winter!"

Followed by *Yet Another Round* of his new game called, "Dad, Dad, Who do you think would win?"

(The rules are simple. Ask Dad who he thinks would win. Propose two options. Tell Dad if Dad's answer was right or wrong!

The following is but a miniscule sampling of the surveys I have undergone whilst locked in these rooms with my boy over the past 4 days...)

"Dad, Dad who do you think would win, Superman or Batman?"

... Batman. "Right."

"Dad, Dad who do you think would win, Bernie or the Pope?"

... Win what?! "Bernie would win!"

"Dad, who do you think would win, A fork or a spoon?"

... I don't know, the fork? - "Right!"

"Dad, who do you think would win, A ball or a football?" ...

Huh? - "The football!"

"Dad, DAD who do you think would win, the Sun or The Hulk?" ....

The Sun?? - "Wrong!"

"Dad, DAD DAD who do you think would win, my foot or my face?"

...Son, I don't understand. - "My face!"

I know *You* read these remarks and your heart is warmed. You think they're cute, I get it. But you have the luxury of *Reading* them, in your own voice - once - and then moving on, perhaps to a far-away, silent corner of your mind where no other voice or sound can reach. Me... No such mercy. I was being bombarded with this game all morning, all afternoon, all evening. It was like Chinese water torture.

Secondly, you have the luxury of a full tank of patience as you read them. Patience, that battle-hardened quality every, I mean *Every* parent, needs to develop in order to make it through each day without breaking a *Lot* of things. Patience, of which every parent quickly learns is a lot like a tank of gas - it is an exhaustible resource. And many days, it will run out! When it does, you're screwed!

Patience officially turned to fumes in my being on Saturday at around 11:30 a.m., somewhere between the questions, "Dad, *Dad*, who do you think would win, Minions with their Fart Machine or Dr. Seuss?" and "Dad, what would you do if a piece of bread came to life with arms and hands and started running around the house?"

I told you, *Robin Williams on LSD*. I wanted to shoot myself.

This must be why someone invented the Serenity Prayer.

Now, lest you think I'm a parenting wimp, WRONG. I'm a battle tested veteran. I've been a stay-at-home father for five years now. I live on the front lines Monday thru Sunday! Battle-hardened stay-at-home moms are my comrades. So I'm hard, but somedays, I just want a way out.

Maybe it got worse because lately my son is prone to continually circling me. Tightly. Orbiting my body so close that I have to say, "Will, h-o-n-e-y, please back up, because you're stepping on my toes."... Yes, 7 year old boys show their love by proximity and word count. I get it.... But I'm a quiet, writer type and I feel like a monk at a Metallica concert.

At about 5 p.m., my son and I are driving to the fish store, and he is talking and talking and talking *and* talking *and* talking, about past, present, future and Dr. Doofenshmirtz, and dinosaurs, and Home Alone, and Legos, and Minecraft, and our pets, and Bernie, and fish, and possible fish names, and The Odd Squad, and bagels, and God knows what else because I'm just trying to hold my shit together and keep faking interest with "Mmm," "Interesting," "Yes," "I don't know,"—when suddenly I look up and see a Wine and Liquor Store, something I never go in, a dirty place I think of for alcoholics—but I *So Wanted to Go In.*

I would have, anything to dull the sound, but for a small voice inside me, still fighting to be heard over the clamor that whispered, "No. NO! Way over the line! Suck it up Patrick. Drinking, is NOT an option—Till he's in bed."

I come home from the fish store and find throw up on the kitchen floor—green leafy hurl—because our asshole cats chewed up the plant my son was growing for a school project.

I have to clean the litter box and make dinner, unpack the groceries, unload and load the dishwasher, help name the new fish, remind my son to not circle me so closely, play 19 more rounds of "Dad, Dad, Who Would Win?" *and* 3 rounds of Hide and Seek—which ends because I step in a small lake of dog pee.

Make no mistake, I want to return all the pets to their rightful adoption shelters. But there's no time, because I have to get my son ready for bed, and read him a book, and answer the question, "Dad, do you think we should name the new fish Rainbow or Rainbow Road?" for which my internal answer is "I don't give a shit," but my external answer is, "I don't know son, what do you think?" for which his external reply is, "Dad who do you think would win, Rainbow fish or a Shark?"

This is an Emergency! Somebody, please, quickly put an IV of wine into my arm!

My nervous system's flashing red. I'd kill for a happy hour. I've failed to be a really loving, fun, good natured dad today. I've faked kindness since morning. My only victory is not being a complete a-hole to an innocent 7 year old, very sweet, boy who completely lacks all ability to read another person's social cues.

5

I tuck my son into his Star Wars sheets and give him a kiss—while secretly, internally counting down the seconds till I can be alone in silence with a drink in each hand. But he's not done talking...

"Dad,"

"What Will??"

"I love you."

And there it is. The reason I wouldn't trade the job of Dad for anything in the world. But Dear God, please turn this water into wine.

The Warden

You didn't say no to what my mom told you to do. If you did there would be consequences. And not the natural consequences a lot of parenting methods of today suggest like, "Oh son you didn't clean your room like I asked so the ants in your room are the natural consequence of leaving your dishes in there forever." No not like that at all. My mom's consequences were like, "Oh you didn't do what I asked you to do? Okay you're grounded for a month, no TV, no friends over, no going to friends, extra chores, starting with move the wood pile and clean the shed after you do the dishes. Next time you'll do the dishes when I ask." I once got grounded for many, many months or as my mother put it, "Until you graduate," but that's another story. Anyhow, you did what my mom told you to do.

I was an eighth grader when my mother gathered my brother and me into the front room of our mobile home and announced, "Boys, I'm going to Texas to visit your aunties and cousins for three weeks. You should come with me and spend time with your family. If you choose not to, then you can stay home with your Grandma. But you should come."

This was perhaps the most incredible sentence I'd

ever heard my mother say because of the simple fact that it included in it, a choice. I couldn't believe my mother was offering us a choice of whether or not to go with her. We'd already done a year in Texas when I was in seventh grade and I had no desire to return to the land of scorpions, centipedes, and shit kickers (a term for boots not Texans).

Texas had actually been good to me in seventh grade. During my six months in Houston, I swapped my first love letters with Maria Husted who boldly went so far as to say she wanted to spend the night with me! (Did I mention we were both in seventh grade?) And in Amarillo, I'd gotten my first kiss from Irma Escobedo, the older woman next door, a eighth grader.

I had such a huge crush on Irma, a beautiful Mexican girl with big dimples, a great body, and a smoking habit. But it ended in tragedy. Just a short while after kissing her she came over, sat me down on the curb after dark, and informed me, "I'm running away. This will be our last time together."

She seemed serious and I broke into crying. Irma, reached behind her neck, unhinged her necklace and presented it to me. It was a 14k gold-plated KISS necklace. As in the band. "You can have this to remember me by," she said feeling bad that I was sobbing.

Irma was gone the next day. She actually did it and I never saw her again. But I still have her necklace.

"What's it going to be son? Texas with me or stay home with your brother and grandmother?"

I told my mother I was going to stay home, "Grandma needs me here."

"Okay son, it was your choice," she replied somewhat chillingly.

My mother left for Texas. The freedom I had secured by my choice was exhilarating. The warden was gone and the prison doors were left open! The only security guard now was my grandmother, bless her heart, and I could easily hoodwink her for whatever purpose necessary. She was practically bedridden. For the first time in my life, my time was truly my own! My brother Mike, a ninth grader, was equally enthused.

The next day, after a nice long sleep in, I exited our front door prepared to spend the whole day away from our home indulging as many teenager fantasies as possible. In other words, I had no real plans but I had the general idea to enroll my best friend in helping me execute the best plans we could come up with together.

The screen door of our mobile home squeaked to a close behind me as my feet stepped down our rickety, brown, front-porch steps. Then I saw it immediately. There was no way not to see it. A huge mountain of dirt right in the middle of our dirt driveway. Like a small Everest. It was all at once unusual, unexpected, intriguing, and shocking. Where did it come from? Why is it here? What the hell? A mountain of dirt taller than me.

I scaled to the top of it. I could see a football I'd been looking for on the roof of our mobile home. I could see over the fence into our neighbor's yard. Unlike us, they had grass. We just had dirt surrounding our mobile home. Maybe the mountain of dirt was for our neighbor since they were always out improving their yard. Maybe it had been delivered to the wrong driveway. The only other possibility I could think of was that my mother had ordered it because she was always talking about planting a garden. But she'd be gone for the next 3 weeks so that didn't make sense, unless it was delivered to our home early. Worst case scenario, mom wanted us to start that garden when she returned home. I didn't want to help make a garden and hoped it was for the neighbors.

"Boys, that dirt pile is not there by accident. You chose to stay home instead of coming to Texas so I ordered it for you," my mother said to my brother and me over the phone. "I thought you could you use a project to keep you busy while I'm gone." The warden was more cunning than I had known. "Sons, I need you to spread that dirt out all evenly around our back yard and front yard. I need you to raise the level of our yard."

Raise the level of our yard?! My beautiful first day of freedom was turning into a nightmare.

I spoke, "Mom! Are you kidding me?! That's a huge mountain of dirt!"

"I'm not kidding Patrick. Do I ever joke about chores?" she replied.

She *never* joked about chores.

"Mom, you want us to spread this dirt all over our yard, but we don't have a yard we just have dirt around our trailer. Are you suggesting we add dirt onto our dirt? Why would we do that?"

"Why would you do that son? Because I told you to, that's why!" As she spoke her reply, I mouthed the words as if they were my own because I'd heard them so many times growing up. "And yes, son, that's what I'm telling you that you have to do. When you're done, then you can have free time. But no free time until you're done or when I get home you'll be grounded - for a long, long time. Your Grandma is reporting to me. Now I suggest you get started."

"We don't have a wheelbarrow. Can't," I quickly replied, happy that I'd thought of a way out just in time.

"I bought you one. You'll find it in the back of the van. Goodbye boys," she said with a discernible sense of self-satisfaction.

In the lottery that is parents, I got a Mexican single mom, who by night was a nurse struggling to make ends meet, and who by day shifted rapidly back and forth between loving mother and strict authoritarian.

She saw the duality in herself and she'd often say to my brother and me, "I have to be a mother and a father." Apparently she thought fathers mostly assigned their children hard-labor, so my brother and I did more than our fair share of hard work growing up, but this was a whole new level. I had to move the mountain, there was no getting out of it. So I began on my own.

I pulled the brand new yellow wheel barrow from the back of our orange and white V.W., found a shiny new shovel with it as well, and a pair of work gloves. My mother had planned this with much forethought.

I sliced the shovel into the side of the mountain and transferred my first scoop into the wheelbarrow. As the dirt hit the metal, I plotted my revenge. I'll work fast and we can finish this by the end of the day. That'll show her.

My grandmother watched through the mobile home window. I had never shoveled dirt into a wheel barrow before. The shovelfuls were heavy but manageable. I was emboldened by how easy it was going to be... until I tried to move my first wheelbarrow load of dirt. Grabbing the two white wheelbarrow handles and lifting gave me a small panic. The wheelbarrow was heavy as $@#! I could barely balance it. Keeping it from falling over to either side was a major victory for my two skinny arms.

But pushing the wheelbarrow forward was a quick defeat. It wouldn't budge. The front tire had sunk into the dirt under all the weight it now carried. I threw my weight into the push, but I couldn't have been more than 110 pounds and it was very likely that the wheelbarrow now outweighed me. I pulled and pushed it out of its stuck position and suddenly it sprung into a forward roll and I was trying to keep up and hold it steady.

I made it seven or eight steps before the wheelbarrow crashed to the left and spilled its contents. Okay, that's where the first load of dirt goes, I decided. This was going to be much harder than I thought.

My brother and I worked all day under central Oregon's hot, high desert sun. Every shovelful feeling like a ten pound weight. Every full wheelbarrow feeling like a load of bricks. Every wheelbarrow movement feeling like a potential train wreck. It was exhausting. It was the hardest thing I'd ever done in my life. And it was only day one.

At the end of the first day, I had a horrifying new understanding about a mountain of dirt - there is far more dirt in it than meets the eye. Far more. Far, far more because of the circumference. The closer you get to the ground, the more mountain there is to move. Those bottom three or four feet - those few feet contain 90% of the mountain. Each wheelbarrow load hardly made a dent.

I worked day after day after day after day with my brother moving the mountain as part of my mother's summer prison program. She was six states away but she owned me. I'd wrap up each day on the chain gang by 4 p.m., completely exhausted and desperate for sleep.

My grandmother had huge dinners waiting and she'd serve them with a large heaping of sympathy. "My daughter is too hard on you!" she'd grumble.

After about a week, the mountain was finally gone. But the next day another mountain of dirt was in the driveway awaiting us. The warden was merciless.

By the time the second mountain was moved, I had only a handful of free days before the warden returned but I was too tired to do much with them. I bet I put on 5 pounds of muscle in those two weeks spreading new dirt around the dirt yard that surrounded our mobile home.

I wanted a new parent by the time my mother returned from Texas. The warden surveyed the work and morphed back into the loving mother. "Good job boys. I knew you could do it."

I had a sense of accomplishment about moving the two mountains but it was tinged with resent. Why did I get such a hard driving, awful parent?

My mother had another surprise in store. She took me to the local hardware store. Bend, Oregon had only one at the time and we had frequented it our entire lives. At one point in my childhood we lived about a mile away from it and my mother would send my brother and me there on our bikes with a list of things we needed for small repairs. I must have been in first grade, my brother in 3rd when she began sending us. This trip to the Hardware store however was for an item we'd never purchased before, a bag of grass seed.

"Now Patrick, you're going to spread that out all around the area you built up and water it every day son," the warden commanded. At this point, I felt lucky to receive such an easy assignment. My brother got 'chop a full cord of wood' duty.

About two weeks later, the first blades of fresh green grass peeked through the dirt. I absolutely delighted in the sight of it! For me, it was like a miracle. Of course life itself had performed the real miracle, but I felt such a sense of ownership because I had spread the seeds of possibility, watered them daily—and I had moved mountains to make it fertile ground!

As our yard continued to turn lush green, I had a deepening realization that I had turned dirt into beauty.

I had turned nothing into something!

It would take me almost two decades to really see the lessons my mother had taught me with those dirt piles. To establish myself as an inspirational speaker at only 26 years old, I had to overcome a mountain of obstacles. The same was true for my theatre career which I began at 33. But in both endeavors I never gave in when I saw all the things I'd have to overcome. I always thought, "One shovelful at a time."

The older I get, the more I truly admire my mother and her lawn prison project. She had vision and gumption. And she was always looking for ways to improve our home while at the same time to strengthen her boys. Her lawn program did both. Plus it helped her stretch her dollars farther.

Free labor and grass seed, well played Mom. Seriously, it wasn't until I was in my late twenties that I learned about sod. I was dumbfounded. The first thought in my head was, "Are you kidding me? Rich people roll out their lawns? *WTF?!*"

Dead Man
Walkin...

Sometimes things go wrong. And once in a while things go really wrong. That once in a while began for me quite innocently. My girlfriend Deanna left me with one obligation as she headed off for a month of leading a camp for students; mail in her car insurance payment. No problem I said, brushing off the urgency in her voice. She left. I set the envelope on my desk. And well... I forgot about it.

Deanna also gave me permission to drive her car, a still-like-new sporty Toyota Celica, which was very kind of her considering it was her primary asset. She was half-way through her second year of launching a new business and thusly about $20,000 in debt, so the car—as cars often can do—gave her a sense of security and ownership.

Monthly, when she'd face a five figure Visa bill that would make her cry, the $12,000 vehicle would pop into her mind exclaiming, "At least you own me Deanna. And I'm parked right outside, ready to whisk you away any time the pressure gets to be too much!" It was a thought that brought relief, even though she didn't actually own it. She still owed $6000, not to bank, but to her grandma who'd paid for half the car as a Christmas present and fronted the other half as an interest free loan. The car was a symbol of her Grandma's love.

About three weeks into babysitting the car, I went to go somewhere and couldn't find it. It wasn't where I thought I left it, so I figure I must have parked it somewhere else. I walked up and down the block, around the side streets, and then all over a four block radius. The car was nowhere to be found. My hands got sweaty and my shoulders cramped as I imagined the car was towed, or stolen.

I ran back into the house and phoned the police.

"Was my Celica towed?"

I could hear the woman's fingers dancing across the keyboard.

"No, not according to our towing records."

Surely this was a mistake of towing records, I thought, and proceeded to call every tow company in the greater San Diego area. Not one of the twenty two had Deanna's prized possession. My head fell into my hands, as I faced the conclusion that the car had been stolen. Some asshole had come in the night and robbed my girlfriend. Some punk had come and thoughtlessly stripped away the very thing that helped my girlfriend feel better on the days when reaching for her dreams was extremely tough.

I grabbed for the phone again and called the police.

"I'm pretty certain my girlfriend's Celica has been stolen."

"Celica's are the 2nd most popular car to steal in San Diego," said the rough, emotionless voice on the other end.

"What's number one?" I asked.

"SUV's," he said.

Deanna's dream car was an SUV. Either she had really good taste in cars, or really poor taste. I drove an old 77 Ford Grenada.

"Are '77 Grenadas stolen much?"

The officer laughed.

I filed a stolen car report.

I sat at my desk dazed and slouching. When my focus returned, my eyes were staring at an envelope with Deanna's name in the return address. It was the letter to Allstate that she'd asked me to send in three and a half weeks ago. Words in red on the front said 'Renewal Payment.' I felt sick the instant I saw them.

I tore open the envelope, praying the contents inside would be different than my fear. She wouldn't leave me responsible for her annual renewal payment. It had to simply be a monthly payment. She couldn't have left me with the one payment a year you have to make, or you lose your car insurance policy. I pulled the invoice out and read the words in horror. "Policy Expires August 15 at midnight, if payment is not received by Aug 15th." I shot a glance to my desk calendar. It was Aug 18th. I'd just filed a police report that the car was stolen on the 17th.

Two days later, Deanna got off the plane, her face exuding happiness to be home. There was also a tiredness to her walk, evidence of a long and emotionally stirring month. Although I could barely breathe from anxiety, I was glad that I'd waited to tell her the bad news face to face.

As I carried her shoulder bag to baggage claim, my nerves continued to fray. My feet felt like they were in shackles. A deep southern voice in my head kept repeating, "Dead Man Walkin'!"

As we waited for her bags to come up on the carousel, she kept deflecting my questions about what her last two days were like, and annoyingly turning them back onto me. "No, no, no. I can tell you about my days later sweet. I wanna know what you're last two days were like."

She was making me sick to my stomach. "No, no, no, no—I want to know what your last two days with the students were like. Tell me every little detail," I replied, knowing that the bad news would soon erase those recollections, similar to how the magnetic blast from an atom bomb erases all computer memory.

She wouldn't talk about it until we got home, got cozy and shared our news over a nice cup of soothing tea. I couldn't stand it anymore. Every second of not telling her was a second of thinking about telling her, so I blurted out, "Deanna I've got something very tough to tell you." She heard the seriousness in my voice and the ease drained away from her face.

"Your car has been stolen."

Deanna studied my face for a second and then giggled. "Right! You're so lame," she said giving me the same rolled eyes that revealed her fondness for my never-ending attempts to pull her leg.

"Deanna, I'm dead serious. This isn't one of my jokes."

She took a second to more thoroughly study of my face, and as she did, her smile sunk away.

"You better not be joking about this Patrick!"

"I swear I'm not Deanna. I wish I was, *but I'm not.*"

Deanna slipped into a blank, despondent face I'd never seen before. She looked like she was processing news that she has cancer. For a second I was certain the tears were about to flood, but then, without warning, she shook her head, beamed a giant smile to me and said, "Oh well, thank God I have car insurance!"

Right then and there, I realized that revealing one bad bit of news at a time was stupid. You should only bear news one bit at a time if you have a bit of bad news and a bit of good news, or if you have two bits of good news, but if you have two bits of bad news they should both definitely be told at the same time. There is no benefit to breaking up bits of bad news.

"Actually you don't." I said.

"Oh yes I do," she said, but she didn't just say it, she commanded it, because she was already onto me and seemed to believe that she might be able to reverse this whole cosmic blunder with the sheer force of her denial.

"Oh no you don't," I said.

"*Yes I Do* because you sent in the insurance payment like you promised you would."

Why she was torturing me this way, I'll never know. She knew I hadn't sent it in. Heck, she doubted that I would send it in, hence why she was so urgent about her instructions in the first place. If she had been certain that I was the kind of person she could trust with paying a bill, she would have just calmly handed it to me and said, "Would you please mail this for me?" But now she was pretending to have believed me to be completely and totally reliable by feigning certainty that I would have sent it in. I always ramble on like this when I'm feeling really, really, really, bad.

"That's just it. I forgot to send in your payment and your policy expired before the car was stolen."

It's hard to watch the person you truly love break down crying, sobbing, staggering a bit. But that was my punishment. And she cried, and cried, and cried for hours upon hours. It was this crying time that revealed

19

to me just how much her car meant to her—her only security and a sentimental gift from grandma, etc., etc.

I'm not being callous, I felt really, really terrible. It seemed of no consolation to Deanna that I had waited to tell her after camp. Or that I was offering to pay her car. She kept reeling from the shock that she now owed car payments on a car she no longer had.

After the crying slowed down, she got mopey. And then that turned into disbelief. And then that turned into anger. It was like watching someone go through the seven stages of accepting death, really.

She called and told her parents, and they were obviously shaken, mostly by very real possibility that I might be their son-in-law someday. Her father, a retired Marine, a former sheriff, and a current rancher heard the tale and said only, "Geez, now I've heard it all. Sorry Honey, that was a good car." She also called her grandma, despite the fact that I begged her not to break her grandma's heart that way. Grandma, now in her nineties, cried. A new low point for me.

Our apartment grew dark as Deanna lay curled up sobbing on the couch. Always one to try my best to make up for my mistakes, I told Deanna, "I'm going to walk down to Whole Foods and get you chocolate ice cream — chocolate ice cream fixes everything. Do you want that?"

She responded that all she wanted was her car back. Cute of her, really.

I went to Whole Food's anyway trusting that ice cream would help. Plus the air was so heavy in the house it was good to get out from underneath it. Conveniently, Whole Foods is only two blocks from our home, so it took me no time to get there.

As I entered the Whole Foods parking lot, I was tortured by the sight of a blue Toyota Celica that looked like the one Deanna used to own. First, life whacked me across the head, and now I felt like it was toying with me. Great—forever doomed to notice all Celicas until Death Do Us Part, and to resent anybody's utterance of words 'insurance', 'bill', 'payment', 'renewal', and 'Toyota', around Deanna.

On second glance I noticed it looked exactly like the Celica Deanna used to own. In fact, it WAS her car, it had the exact same license plate number!

The thief who stole my girlfriend's car was inside Whole Foods shopping! And I was lucky enough to be in the right place at the right time to be the hero of my own story!

My good fortune was almost unfathomable. But there was no time to think about the odds, I needed to prepare quickly for apprehending the car thief when they emerged from the store. I knew I had to man up, but I knew not a thing about how one does that. I'm a 140 pounds of strapping lack of muscle. But bravely I positioned myself between the car and store's exit doors. My mind began racing with possible scenarios; the thief breaks into a run, or punches me in the face, or draws a knife, or draws a GUN, or...

Wait a minute...

Was it possible I left the car here after picking up a few groceries earlier in the week?

I let that sink in a minute...

It is possible I was driving home, stopped at the store, and then walked home—forgetting that I'd driven there.

It all came flooding back to me.

Yup, *that's what happened!*

No thief.

Just a lot on my mind.

I didn't feel stupid. I felt ecstatic! Exuberant. Elated. Enraptured. I ran home to tell Deanna the good news. She was going to be so thrilled and happy, I just knew it.

I danced and danced in front of her as a warm up act, blocking her view of the TV. She was not showing joy yet. "What the hell are you doing?" She asked disgustedly. "I found your car! I found your car! *I found your car!*" I said while continuing my Snoopy dance. "Yeah, it's at Whole Foods where I parked it!! Go figure, I just forgot I drove it there! Isn't this great!!"

I think her exact words were "That is so $!@#!@$ up!" And if she was happy about the return of her car, her face didn't know about it. And then she said, "Well give me my ice cream."

Foiled again. In my elation I'd forgotten to buy it... What's the matter with me??

"Call your parents right away," I pleaded. "I don't want them to think bad of me any longer than necessary.., or to worry."

It was Deanna's mother who awoke and answered the phone. When Deanna was through with her update (not presented at all in the joyful tone I thought the news deserved), her father woke up and inquired about the call. "Patrick found Deanna's car. He had parked it at the grocery store and forgot it." I could hear the man's two words, even though I wasn't on the phone: "Un$!@#!inbelieveable. Goodnight."

Epilogue—Deanna married me. Can you believe it?

The Birds and
The Bees

Tonight at dinner with my family, I'm telling a story about my mother which involves how my mother was given away as a child because her mother was overwhelmed by trying to raise 4 children on dishwasher wages.

My son, Will, asks, "But what about her husband? Why didn't he help her?"

I say, "Your grandmother didn't have a husband."

Will looked absolutely puzzled. Like someone had just told him they dropped a rock and it fell upwards.

"If she wasn't married then *how* did she have kids?" he asked.

And with that we remember that at 7 years of age, Will's only explanation for where babies come from has thus far been, *you get married and your love makes kids.* Old fashioned, I know. Close to true on the love making part. And prior to this very moment in a Thai Food restaurant, age appropriate.

Anyway, back to the story. The restaurant we're in is so small you might as well be having dinner with everyone sitting at the tables around you—because you can hear everything they're saying and smell their food as if it was on your own table. All things considered, we'd like to deep six Will's question immediately so we're all just taking a moment of... pause.

But Will's on it like a bird dog now.

"Seriously, if she wasn't married then *How* did she have kids?"

My wife steps into the quicksand. "They just did Will because people who are not married also have kids."

Not good enough. "*But How*?!" Will asks again.

Our daughter, 16, is cracking up and turning a bit red. I've gone quiet trying to decide if I should break out the big V and P words.

But then my wife makes a second pass.

"Will, babies are made like this," and her left-hand rises. Using her index finger and thumb, she makes a circle!

I immediately know what the circle represents and I can't believe my wife is going for it! I'm shocked and just waiting for her right hand to rise up with one straight finger headed for the circle, all right over a plate full of Pad Thai!

I did *Not* know she had this level of explanation in her! Nor am I sure it's age appropriate. But at the same time I'm kinda impressed because it is straight to the point.

Wow, my son is about to learn about sex from his mom doing an anatomical demonstration with her hands! In a restaurant! My eyes are opened as wide as Will's, and same goes for my daughter's. Let's just say my wife has everyone's attention.

Then, with the little circle she makes with her left hand, my wife goes, "Will, a woman has an egg."

I about spit out my food realizing that the circle represented an egg... I completely got that wrong! I burst out laughing!

Will exclaims, "Ha! *Mom has eggs!*" That really tickled his funny bone and seems to be all the answer he needs.

My wife completes the brief fertilization talk. Rice becomes the semen. Thanks a lot honey, couldn't you have used a food I didn't eat all the time?

So now my son thinks babies come from putting rice into a women's egg, and he likely thinks those eggs are about three inches around with a hard shell. Oh well, we can fill him on delivery systems the next time we're out to dinner.

Parenting. Totally awesome.

Unreal Blue

Today I was driving back from cleaning up a tree that had fallen at my rental home downtown. I was the third wheel helping the gardeners. I marveled at how skilled they were at their job.

Picture cutting down enough tree limbs, branches, and vines to cover half of an entire basketball court, because we did. And then they methodically chain-sawed it, raked it, bagged it, and stacked it, and stacked it, and stacked it so it all fit into the back of their pick-up truck. They put more fallen tree into the back of a pick-up truck than I could have imagined would fit into cargo ship.

There was something that seemed peaceful, organic, and real about their work. I thought maybe I'd enjoy being a gardener. My job speaking and writing more and more often can seem so self-centered and so self-promotional. But I do it because it's me. It's what I do. It's the space I play in to try and be a helpful human being. But I needed that tree removed just as much as anyone needs another "talk" or "essay."

I'm almost 50. My priorities are changing. I can feel it.

Anyway, on the drive home I pulled into a charging station to recharge my car. I drive an electric. Well, right beside the charging station was a man sleeping on a concrete block. Homeless for sure. I felt bad for him. It looked like an absolutely terrible place to sleep. Hard surface. Hot sun. Roadside fumes. Noise...

I thought about waking him and asking if he was hungry. It takes 30 minutes to charge up, so I thought I could use the wait time to get this man some lunch. All too often I don't help the homeless person I pass. I'm callous. I look away. Not always. But too often. But today, I just wanted to help him somehow.

He was wearing black sweat pants and a blue hoodie. He had gray Converses on. They looked new. The sweat pants and the hoodie, tattered and dirty. He had the hoodie pulled up—I suppose it was playing the part of a blanket—but what struck me about his face was his solid white beard, trimmed very close. I liked his beard. Between his fairly new Converse shoes and his trimmed beard, it seemed like life wasn't completely kicking him in the teeth. I spoke to try and wake him. No response.

I guess he's really drunk and out of it I thought to myself.

I looked around and saw a Mexican food joint a block away, just beyond the Starbucks. Starbucks seems stupid when you're thinking about getting something to help another hungry human being. I go there all the damn time, because my life is luxurious every damn day. But my guess was that this man would appreciate a burrito more than a Grande, double-shot, Caramel Macchiato with extra foam, light ice, and a twist of cinnamon.

I walk over and get the burrito. I'm vegan but deep down inside I believe meat is going to satisfy this guy more than just rice and beans, so I order a carne asada burrito.

I'm remembering as I write this, I've actually handed a homeless person a vegan burrito in the past, and he took one bite out of it, asked where the meat was and handed it back to me with a "no thanks." Yeah, this is no time to promote a vegan diet.

I walk back to him. He's still sleeping. I notice I'm a tiny bit afraid of waking him. What if he jolts awake and screams at me with huge, wide open eyes? What if he immediately grabs my arm and bites my face? What if he's on drugs and mistakes me for an attacking animal? These are the stupid thoughts I have right before I put my hand on his leg and shake him awake.

His eyes open very slowly. Like they haven't opened for years. And then as they achieve their goal, they clearly show that they are very unsure as to what's happening. They are trying to focus on me, to find an answer.

What I notice most is their spectacular blue color. They are the bluest eyes I've ever seen in my 49 years alive. They are like a metallic sky blue on a $50,000 automobile. If this guy was standing next to Paul Newman, no one would notice that Newman's eyes were blue. I am absolutely amazed at these eyes.

"Are you hungry?" I ask.

He nods. And then his eyes find the bag of food I'm offering. It's in one of those flimsy white plastic bags they always give you when you order take out. More plastic to choke the world. Why did I allow them to place one single $!@#!%$ burrito in the plastic bag when I was only going a block..? I must have been thinking about the homeless guy.

He quickly opens the bag and pulls out the burrito. No time for talk, he gets the first bite in his mouth as fast as possible. And then a sip of the drink I brought him, which is water. His eyes glance at me approvingly, but then he begins coughing doubling over to spit. It's like a gag reflex. But he sits up, looks me right in the eyes and rubs his stomach. And then resumes with another enormous bite.

No words from him yet. Not a one.

"Are you okay?" I ask.

He swallows. And then tries to speak.

But I can't make out what he's saying. Maybe his voice is severely muffled. Maybe he is only saying one word. I'm confused. His voice is unexpected.

"What's your name?" I ask.

He extends his left arm and using his finger draws something on his forearm. I don't know what he's doing, so he draws it again. E - D.

"Oh, your name is Ed?"

He nods his head. His blue eyes staring directly into mine. And he continues to eat.

I should have been sure by now, but I'm not.

"Ed, can you speak?"

He shakes his head no and makes a shallow attempt to say it also. But it's clear. Ed has very little ability to speak. But his eye contact is excellent. And his eyes are so, so blue. They are unreal blue.

I felt like sitting there with him. I could have gotten in my car and passed the time on my phone, but I felt like sitting with him. I don't know why. I do know, but it feels like a stupid reason. I'm trying to offer this other person a meal and a little companionship. I didn't just want to offer food. Seems people need both.

Since Ed is eating and not a talker, I manage the situation with silence and only two other remarks.

There is a beautiful large bush in front of us. Most of the leaves are green, but a few new ones are red. It's pretty when you really look at it.

"Beautiful how this bush has red leaves and green ones, don't you think Ed?"

He nods and looks me in the eye.

Then silence while he eats.

"Ed, I asked for chips to go with your burrito but the guy in the shop only put a few in. He was being cheap. But they're in there." I say.

Ed, finds the chips in the white plastic bag. They would have been missed otherwise because they are enclosed separately in a white plastic bag. For $!@#!$ sake! It's killing me. Then Ed unties the small plastic bag and reveals 2 tortilla chips. TWO. —Just two $!@#!#$ chips. Now I remember the man behind the counter looking at me like I was a freeloader when I said, "And can you throw in some chips with the burrito."

Ed is eating the last chip and then excitedly points at something flying by.

It's a radiant yellow butterfly. It looks like a fluttering slice of the sun.

I don't know what a butterfly symbolizes but I see it and wonder.

When Ed is done eating both chips, he points forward at a Starbucks cup thrown on the ground in front of us. He gets up and retrieves it. He places it, the foil, and the napkin in the white plastic bag. He looks at me and smiles. Then he rubs his stomach and smiles more. But he's going now. He attempts to speak again. This time I know what he's saying: "Taking trash."

He grabs the only other bag he's got, a black duffle bag, offers me his hand and goes.

Ed was really hungry. That was easy to see by the pace he ate at and by the first bite going down wrong. I don't know why I don't help homeless people more often. I'm trying to open my heart as wide as I can and I know it has the capacity to be much more open than it is. I know it does. I can feel it. Especially in moments like this.

Call 911!

"Call me an ambulance, I'm pregnant."

It was 7:00 AM, on June 29, 1988, and I was doing what I did five days a week—walking to my internship at Levi Strauss & Co.'s corporate headquarters in beautiful San Francisco. I was 22 years old, a senior in college, and still filled with the excitement a city like San Francisco injects into a young person's veins. Just walking through it always put an extra spring into my step.

On this particular morning, I'd only gone one block from my apartment when I noticed people ahead of me looking down as they passed something lying on the sidewalk. Everyone looked but no one stopped.

When I got to the spot of interest, I saw a young woman and she mouthed something to me. I stopped, removed my headphones and said, "What?"

The young woman with a slightly freckled face said, "Call me an ambulance, I'm pregnant."

She didn't look pregnant, but she looked a bit tattooed and worn down. I figured that was enough reason to call for help so I said OK and began knocking on apartment doors.

The third door I knocked on opened. An older African-American man heard me out and agreed to let me use his phone.

911 asked me if she was pregnant. I told them I wasn't sure. They asked me if she was crowning. I said, "What's crowning?!" They said it's when you can see the baby's head emerging. I said, "I had no idea." They indicated they'd send an ambulance.

I hung up the phone and stepped back outside to inform the sidewalk woman. Standing there in slacks, white shirt and tie, and holding my black briefcase, I said "The ambulance is on its way. Are you going to be alright, because I need to go to work now?"

I was just about to get back on my way when she replied, "While you were inside, my water broke!"

I looked down at her old blue jeans and sure enough, they were soaking wet. Either her water did break which meant she actually was pregnant, or she peed... I chose to believe the former, so I put down my briefcase.

Suddenly there I was on the sidewalk of Fell Street—a busy, four-lane street in San Francisco—faced with a human being who really seemed desperate. She was actually lying down on steps that descended into a doorway just below street level.

The first thing I decided to do was grab her by her shoulders and move her fully onto the sidewalk. Then I pictured she might start having the baby soon and I imagined it not being able to come out because of her jeans. So I said, "I'm going to take your pants off."

She didn't reply so I took that as an "okay." I figured on leaving her underwear safely on. Then... I took off her pants. Turns out she wasn't wearing any underwear.

Suddenly she was in pain, trying to curl up, and her hand was clawing across the cement. My next move was obvious—I reached up, grabbed her hand, and held it.

I put my other hand on her shoulder to try and keep her lying flat. This poor woman was in so much pain. I tried to talk to her a bit by asking her name. She quickly said it was "Bobbie".

"Hi Bobbie. My name is Patrick." I filled time by asking more questions that she didn't bother to answer. Questions like, "How are you feeling now? Are you OK? Do you live around here?"

Her free hand suddenly flew to her crotch. Apparently attempting to hold the baby in--at least that's what I thought. I grabbed her hand and said, "Bobbie, don't try to hold the baby in, okay? I'm sure it's not good to try and hold the baby in."

Then I said, "I think you'll know when you're going to have the baby and when you do, just tell me, okay? We can have a baby on the sidewalk."

I was saying this strictly as words of encouragement because in my mind I pictured the ambulance arriving any minute.

Bobbie didn't reply but she stopped trying to hold the baby in with her hand.

By now several people were gathered about 10 feet behind me watching. I was hoping one of them would come up and offer help, but they didn't budge, and since things seemed to be under control I didn't ask.

I went back to talking to this half-naked young woman I was beginning to feel a strong bond with. She wouldn't say a thing. She had contractions to deal with.

Someone tapped me on the shoulder. "Another helper!" I thought, but no... It was woman who'd only come forward to insist that I cover her crotch with a blanket.

"Cover her up," she said with a tone of disgust and quickly retreated. To hell with covering her up, I thought as I tossed the blanket back off. I wanted to be able to see what was going on in the region that currently mattered the most.

Next thing I know, a fast-talking woman in a bright red dress was talking to Bobbie! She knew Bobbie! I felt so relieved!! A friend of Bobbie's! She was standing just above Bobbie's head and she was firing off frantic remarks.

"Bobbie, whatareyoudoing!? Whatthe$!@#!s goingongirl?! Bobbie, are you havin' a baby??! I didn't know you were pregnant. Damnthisaintright. Weneedhelp. Ican'tstandthis. Bobbieyoucan'thaveababyonthesidewalk!!"

A barrage of increasingly frantic comments kept flying out of the woman's mouth. This was not the help I'd hoped for! Just when I was at a loss for how to respond to the situation, Bobbie helped out. She looked straight up at the woman and said, "Dianne, Shut the $!@#! up!" Shortly thereafter, Dianne exited the scene.

I however didn't notice her disappearance because shortly after Bobbie spoke to her friend, she spoke to me in a calm but certain voice, "I'm going to have the baby now."

The power behind those seven words, "I'm going to have the baby now," forced me to think fast. I had no idea what to do. But I'd told Bobbie that we could have a baby on the sidewalk. It was obvious, I now needed to live up to that casual remark that I'd intended to be comforting, not procedural.

Although I was very embarrassed to do it, I moved in between Bobbie's legs and put my hands out. I looked down at my hands, and, regrettably on their own, they

35

had mimicked the hands of a quarterback ready to take the snap. Then I started talking, "Okay Bobbie, Breathe! Push! Breathe! Push! You can do it!!" And then I stole a glimpse—glanced quickly to try and see a baby's head. I saw a six inch strip of something deep purple, and suddenly thought to myself—Oh that's crowning!

What I didn't know was if I was seeing the baby's head or the "placenta". This was that moment when I realized I didn't know which came out first. Somewhere in my past I'd learned the concept of placenta. But not the timing of it. And now suddenly I really wanted to know if placenta comes before or after the baby, because if it came first I didn't want it all over my hands.

Yeah, that's the messed up thoughts that were running around in my head.

Bobbie was breathing -- fast and furious. And I can assure you that her efforts to breathe had nothing to do with my reminders. In between frantic breaths she'd strain to push. She took a deep, deep breath, and then while screaming in pain, she gave an enormous push—POP!!

Suddenly I was staring at a baby head! It had just popped out—without any warning or passage of time. It was just there!

And for the first time, a panicked thought exploded in my mind, "What do I do?? Am I supposed to pull the baby out now that I can grab onto the head? Or am I NOT supposed to pull? "What do Doctors do!?"

I'd seen birthing scenes at least twenty times on television, but until now I hadn't realized that those TV scenes were leaving out VERY important details. The doctor just reaches under a blanket and then *shazam*, they produce a baby like a magician pulling a rabbit from a hat.

Without knowing what to do, I reached out with both hands to touch the baby's head—and when I did, I was treated to a small miracle.

The instant my fingers touched the baby's tiny head I was filled up with a knowingness: You don't pull the baby out. You just be there, to catch it. Suddenly knowing what to do was a miracle to me! It was as if life itself had whispered the answer into my ear.

I went back to the only real job I had—"Breathe! Push!! Breathe Bobbie!! Push! You're doing great!!" Bless her heart, Bobbie was doing all the work. She built herself up again for another mighty push and—SLIP-SLOSH-SLIP! Out slid the second third of the baby from the neck to knees. Slipped out just like a little wet noodle and made a sloshing sound along the way.

To see this newborn baby emerge was ecstasy to me. I began screaming with excitement to Bobbie, "You did it!!! We have a little girl!!! Bobbie you are the best! The best! I love you!" And then I gently pulled the baby all the way out. I had a little blue baby in my hands, from head to toes.

In my excitement, I hadn't noticed that the baby was in fact a deep shade of bluish-purple. But suddenly I noticed and got the horrible feeling that this little girl wasn't alive. Words can't describe the terrifying thoughts that took over my mind. How can life go from that exuberant to that frightful so quickly? There were twelve bystanders watching safely from a distance. They'd chosen not to get involved. Me, I was deeply involved.

In a moment that I'll remember at the end of my life, I was looking down on the still and lifeless face of this baby, trying to say words that might bring the baby girl around. I gave her a little shake and her two little baby eyes opened up.

First they looked to the left, at the traffic of Fell Street speeding by. Then they looked to the right, at the Victorian houses. And then they looked straight up at me, and I was all smiles and screams.

I gave the newborn a gentle shake and out came a cry, and a gasp. At that moment, all I wanted was more gasps and cries, so I kept giving the baby little shakes. And the more the little girl would cry, the more her skin grew pink with life.

"You did it Bobbie! We've got a beautiful, alive, baby girl!!"

I just held the baby right there in the spot where she'd come from. It was less than a minute when I noticed, out of the corner of my eye, the flashing red, blue, and orange lights of an ambulance.

I saw the paramedic coming toward me, flashed on what he must be thinking at the sight of me holding a newborn, and filled up with a sense of pride. I thought I might be in line for a Citizen's Award. But the first thing he said to me was, "Don't elevate the baby's head like that. You're holding it wrong."

The next thing he did surprised me even more—he handed the infant up to Bobbie's arms, and for the first time I realized that the umbilical cord can stretch quite a ways. Picture a coiled phone cord, because that's exactly what it looks like. I would have handed Bobbie her baby if I'd realized it stretched. Heck, I might have tried to take the baby in the house for warmth.

I don't know what the paramedics did next.

I sat down on a sidewalk ledge and began shaking uncontrollably. I wanted to talk to Bobbie, but she was out of it. I wanted to know what hospital they were taking her to, but I couldn't concentrate on their answer. I did notice a bag of clothing where Bobbie had been lying, so I gave it to the paramedics. And then I just resumed sitting and shaking.

The neighbor who'd let me call 911 from his phone sat down beside me. He put his hand on my shoulder and said, "Bet you could use a good stiff drink right now. Come on inside and sit down for a while." This was a nice man.

I opted for tea, and as he prepared it we discovered that we shared the same birthday, July 5. Then it hit me—today was my Mother's birthday. I had to call her and I began the call by saying, "Happy Birthday Mom. Have I got birthday news for you—you're a grandmother!"

She demanded an immediate explanation.

Instead of taking the MUNI train to work, I walked the four miles. Well, more specifically I would walk a block and then burst into an excited skip-like jump with my arms swinging. I was so thrilled.

I got to work over an hour late, but I didn't care, I had the world's greatest excuse. First I told the administrative assistant, "Guess what I did this morning..." Then someone wandering by insisted that I repeat the story so that they could hear the beginning. Then my boss, Sydney, wanted to hear the story.

I told the story over and over. And some people would listen to it twice. After about an hour of this, Sydney, called me into her office. It was pretty easy to guess that she was calling me in to tell me it was time to STOP telling the story and get to work. She said, "Patrick, your story is wonderful and I was wondering if I could call my friend at the San Francisco Chronicle and tell it to him?"

"Sure," I replied.

The reporter from the Chronicle seemed to like the

story and asked Sydney if she'd let me off work so that the paper could take my photo on the site where it happened. She obliged and gave me the rest of the day off!

Sure enough, an hour later I was standing there on the sidewalk, where you could see a small spot of blood, posing for a newspaper photographer.

The next morning I was awoken extra-early by the ringing of my phone. Completely under the influence of sleep, I answered the phone almost angrily. In the most bright and cheery voice you can imagine, the man on the line said, "Hello, we're looking for Patrick Combs. Is this Patrick?"

"Yes," I said.

"Congratulations Dr. Combs! This is K101 radio and we're thrilled about what you did yesterday. Did we wake you?"

"Uh huh," I droned.

"You sound sleepy. Should we call you back in 15 minutes so you have some time to shower and grab a cup of coffee?—and perhaps deliver another baby?"

"Yes please," said I.

And they did call me back. They had a local band sing a song they'd composed on the fly for me. I couldn't believe it.

It was time to go to work. As I was exiting my apartment building, a man who was entering stopped me and said, "Patrick, right? I'd just like to shake your hand and say congratulations. That was a very nice thing you did."

I had *No* idea who this man was and being recognized by a stranger was very disorienting. "How did you know what I did?" I asked.

He held up the newspaper and said, "You made the front page of the Chronicle." Sure enough, there was my picture, front and center, above the fold.

Seeing myself right underneath the San Francisco Chronicle masthead was like being hit with a stun gun. The headline said, "San Francisco State Student Delivers a Baby on the Sidewalk."

I read the article and discovered two things: Bobbie named the baby Krystal, and Bobbie was in fact, Bonnie. I had misheard her name the first time.

This was the second strange trip to work I'd had in a row. As I walked to the train, I'd pass newspaper boxes with my picture staring out. As I was riding the train, I was surrounded by people reading a story about me.

The minute I got to the door of Levi Strauss & Co., the excitement escalated. The security officer at the door said, "You need to get upstairs fast. They're waiting for you."

Upstairs, my boss Sydney rushed me into her office and started explaining. There were lots of television and radio stations that wanted to interview me, and, Robert Haas, the President of Levi Strauss & Co., wanted me to stop by his office and tell him the story.

I did a full day of radio and televisions interviews, including a live television show appearance on San Francisco's People Are Talking. I saw many smiles and tears of joy in the audience as I related my story with great enthusiasm.

The next day a news crews wanted to escort me to the hospital where Bonnie was staying. They wanted a big reunion scene. I said no to the idea. I wanted to preserve Bonnie's privacy. I entered her hospital room alone, anxious to see her, form a bond, and of course see our baby girl.

Bonnie, looking beat down by life and older than me, cut right to the chase, "I guess I'm supposed to say thank you because you're a hero. Well, thank you. You have all the fun you want with this, but I ain't doing no interviews." She seemed angry. The media attention probably bothered her. But I sensed that under the surface, she was battered, bitter, and embarrassed about being homeless.

I felt horrible for showing up. How could I have thought it would be anything but like this? I said very little - only that I understood and wished her well. *I didn't get to see Krystal.*

The next day I made an appearance on The Late Show with Joan Rivers, in Los Angeles. A comedian named Ross McGowan was filling in for Joan. He called me out of the audience as a surprise guest. I still shared the story with an honest joy, as it was the most beautiful happening yet in my life. Again the audience genuinely enjoyed the story, smiling, laughing, and even crying.

In the weeks after, I received cards and letters from people who'd read my story in the newspaper -- imagine my surprise when I realized one of them was from Alice Walker, the author of The Color Purple. Her words were incredibly kind.

A year passed before I heard anything of baby Krystal and her mother Bonnie. I had concluded that I'd lost track of them forever. But then one afternoon my phone rang and a woman introduced herself as the person who had adopted Krystal.

She informed me that Krystal had gone straight up for adoption. She said she was calling to let me know that despite worries that Krystal might be a crack baby (because of the extremely fast birth), she was in fact a perfectly healthy and happy child.

"And how is Bonnie?" I asked.

"I'm sorry to say that Bonnie died of an overdose last December," she said. I felt a stabbing pang of sadness and regret in my heart. I wished I would have found a way to make sure Bonnie was okay. I had woefully overlooked her plight.

I asked if I could see Krystal.

The woman said, "No."

She said they weren't sure if they would ever tell her about her sidewalk birth and that her name was no longer Krystal. They had renamed her.

For the life of me I couldn't remember the new name they'd given her by the time the call was over, maybe because I didn't want to. The way I saw it, her birth mother gave her two gifts, birth and a name.

I wonder if someday without even knowing it, I'll pass the little girl I helped bring into this world while walking down some street. Or if someday, life will magically connect us again. In any case, I'm deeply grateful that I didn't walk on past or stand safely back as a bystander on that fateful day that I encountered Bonnie asking for help, and instead followed my heart's desire to bring comfort to a person in need. It gifted me one of the greatest joys of my life.

Audition

"Dad! I got invited to a movie audition. Should I go? Can I go?"

My daughter's dream is acting in movies. She is staring at her computer which is open to the acting profile she keeps on Backstage.com, a movie industry site.

This is the first audition invite from Hollywood she's ever received.

"Holy heck Alyssa, that's wonderful, read it to me!"

It's from a director at the American Film Institute for a short movie. AFI is a really big deal. We google to find that out and we're both kinda stunned when we do.

"What should I write back? Could I go to Los Angeles for an audition?" she asks.

My daughter has dreamed of acting in movies since she could talk.

We work out a reply and press send.

The next day, she gets another message from the director inviting her to audition on Wednesday at 7:30. Just five days away.

I believe in my daughter's dream of acting. I always have. I believe in my daughter. And I believe in those whispers that tell us what we'd really love to do in our lives.

Alyssa has long amazed me with how she silently and effectively goes about the care taking of her dream, almost never asking for help.

The director sends her a bit of the script, the movie is named Eyes of Dawn. It's about a teenage girl who's bullied at school and lives at home with an alcoholic dead-beat dad. Alyssa does school plays and she never reads her lines out loud for her parents. We always see it first at the live performance. But this time, I say, "Want to run lines with me? Since I'm a dad." She says "Sure". I'm surprised and happy to be sitting in front of the fireplace reading script lines back and forth with my daughter for the first time ever.

In the script I get to yell, "Go to your room!" We say not a word about it, but we both know how I sound when I say the line in real life. Now she gets a new line to respond with, "It's a little too late for that." We run the lines about ten times. She's doing great.

Alyssa needed this break. This audition. Just last month, she lost the lead role she really wanted in a high school play and instead got what she felt was a bit part. I picked her up from school the day she got the news and she could barely speak the whole drive home. I think she wanted to cry. It was my first time as a father watching my kid suffer the disappointment of your dream not going as you so badly wanted, as you so badly felt you needed.

I had words of advice that were born out of my own disappointments in not being picked, of not getting the gig, of feeling overlooked and not good enough. But for the first time as I shared them with my daughter, I felt like a lousy inspirational speaker. I could see my daughter still felt defeated.

I took her for a treat. That, a hug, and family seemed

to work better than words of wisdom. Just having family that loves you no matter what seemed to be far better than any words.

Three days to go before the audition. Alyssa tells me something when she gets in the car after school.

"My drama teacher was so excited about my audition she dedicated the entire class to helping me get ready. And tomorrow she's going to do the same!"

I hear this and feel enormous gratitude, to the teacher of course, God bless the teacher for such graceful and generous kindness. But I also feel grateful to the entire Universe. I want a friendly Universe for my daughter. I want the entire Universe to conspire for her to have a positive experience with her dreams.

Two Days Before the Audition

We call my close and long-time friend Ken, an Emmy-award winning director and 20 year Hollywood veteran.

He gets on the phone with Alyssa—who has never done any movie audition before. Ken says, "The most important thing is to go in there and enjoy it. Have fun! You're auditioning at AFI and you're doing what you love. So don't concern yourself with getting the part. Just enjoy yourself all the way."

As he speaks to Alyssa over speaker phone, I see my life choices and my friends now benefiting my daughter's life, and I am amazed. Never saw that coming. My friend of decades is now mentoring my daughter.

The Day of Audition

It's my job to print out her first headshot. Her friend

Lilly took it. When it comes out of the Kinko's photo machine, I'm amazed. My daughter looks every bit a beautiful young woman but the photo isn't what I expected. She's smiling in it. But not a full smile. And her eyes, they say, "I'm friendly, but I am serious."

She only needs one head shot. I print a second one for my wall.

3:30 p.m.

It's time to pick Alyssa up and drive to Hollywood. Her audition is at 7:30. Hollywood is a 2 hour drive. We should have plenty of time to get there, but it's *Pouring Rain*. This isn't just a hard San Diego rain. It's a freak storm sent by Mother Nature to say, "You bet your ass climate change is real, and today I'm sending a warning to all my little friends in San Diego". I mean it's coming down Biblically.

I don't say anything. But I know this rain will massively slow down the drive to Los Angeles. This could make us late.

And then, both of our phones sound an emergency alert. And display a warning that certainly has never happened before in San Diego: *Tornado Warning!*

What?!

It seems almost impossible. We live in a beach town.

God. Please. Not tonight.

While we're driving in this torrential downpour I make another call. "Ransford, please pick up," I think to myself. Ransford is the only working actor I know. Met him last year when he became a speech coaching client. Super nice guy with enough energy to power a small city. I would love Alyssa to get a bit of advice from him.

He answers!

Ransford talks to my daughter. Among a stream of great advice, the one that hits my daughter the most is, "Alyssa, just go in there and tell the story. You're not there to audition. Or for them to like you. You're just there to tell the story. They already saw something they like in you, that's why they asked you to audition. Now they're just hoping you can help them tell the story." I watch this advice both relax and excite Alyssa. She feels ready. And she keeps saying she feels ready.

I have a surprise for the drive planned.

"Hey, I thought we could listen to the actor Rob Lowe's audiobook. He's got a chapter where he tells the story of auditioning at your age for The Outsiders."

The weirdest thing I did in December is buy and listen to Rob Lowe's audiobook. I thought I didn't like Rob Lowe. But then one little excerpt—I heard almost accidentally—and I buy the thing and listen to it all. I kept saying to friends, "I'm doing the weirdest thing. I'm listening to Rob Lowe's audiobook. *I even paid money for it*. I don't even know if I like Rob Lowe..."

Well I ended up liking his audiobook very much. But now as it's playing for my daughter, and he's saying things like, "I don't think actors are great liars. I think great actors are actually great truth tellers. The tellers of their truth, what's true for them in the words on the script." I love Rob Lowe, and I want to give him a huge hug.

The car navigation system keeps pushing our arrival time back. Now it tells us we're going to make it to the audition at 7:20. If Rob wasn't telling us a story, we'd really be sweating it. We're sweating it anyway. We're just staying positive about the situation.

But we're not going to make it on time.

Unless the rain stops.

There's no sign of it stopping.

Mother Nature seems like she's just getting started.

And then, the rain stops. Just goes away. Like a miracle.

We make it to AFI at 7:03. Uncle Rob shared Hollywood stories and advice with us for most of the ride.

We park at the American F-ing Film Institute. I know this is where my daughter gets out of the car, and I'm supposed to be the cool dad who waits outside. I know she doesn't want her Dad to be seen anywhere near her first Hollywood audition. I know. But I *so very much* wish I could go in. I so very much wish she wasn't 16 yet. I so very wish she was 12 or 13 or even 14 and still wanted me to go with her because I want to be there supporting her. But I know. I know I have to let her go. She's 16.

"Okay honey, go in there and have fun. I know you'll be wonderful and I'll be here waiting!" I say.

"Dad, I'm sure you can come in with me," she says, asking.

I wrote this whole story to tell you that line.

I just broke out of story to tell you how much her saying that meant to me.

She *wanted* me to come in with her.

She still *needs* me.

I'm still her Dad.

This is for me, a beautiful moment.

I'm new to being a father. Almost every day being a parent is a new experience. I've never had a 16 year old daughter before. I myself never had a dad. My daughter has never been on this step into her own life, into her dreams, into the actual world. And I'm making it up as I go. Every step of the way. All the time. Constantly. Every new situation, I'm just guessing at how to be a good Dad. Aren't we all?

I'm sure it meant almost nothing that she wanted me to come with her, but to me, it meant the world because she's almost grown. And I've got so little time left with her. And I hope I haven't messed up too much. I hope I've done enough. I hope I've been okay as a father. And maybe this is a small sign that I've done enough right.

"Oh! Ok, great! Let's go in," I say. She has no idea.

We go in to AFI. This is hallowed ground. The walls are covered with black and white photographs of AFI award winners and graduates. It is the Who's Who in Hollywood directing, producing, editing, cinematography and screenwriting. Giant movie posters also adorn the walls, each declaring with placards the AFI graduates who were involved in making that movie.

My daughter's first audition, at AFI. This is beyond legit. Thank you God!

In the hallways actors are already gathered and waiting, my daughter's competition. Like my daughter, they're all dressed the part. Leather jackets. Doo rags. Torn jeans. Flannel shirts. I'm wondering, "Is my daughter freaking out?" She looks pretty cool and confident. As a matter a fact, she's got this HUGE smile on her face, she's so excited. Like best day of her life excited. "How is she not freaking out?" I wonder.

We sit in little chairs against the hallway walls near the other actors. I lean into Alyssa and whisper, "Remember, don't smile so much because you're playing a girl who's sad and angry."

She notices that she is in fact smiling like a school

girl with a huge crush and nods. Then the smile disappears. Good acting.

The director, a young woman who all at once seems friendly, professional and impressive calls in the first actor.

The teenage girl goes in and the unexpected happens. Alyssa and I hear her audition through the walls!

Oh that's not good, I think to myself. Even Rob Lowe says the last thing an actor wants is to have to see other people's auditions. Francis Ford Coppola casted like that and Rob said it was terrifying. But Alyssa keeps giving me looks to assure me that she's okay. She's feeling good.

I'm so proud of her.

And then, 30ish minutes later, the director calls my daughter into the room.

And the door closes.

Now, she's on her own.

And Dad can only wait. And hope.

Please God, it's her first audition. Let it be a positive experience. Please God, let her walk out of that room happy. Let her walk out of there feeling that she did good.

One more girl is in the hall waiting to audition. I decide to say hello.

"Hi, do you do a lot of these?" I say.

I worried I might be interrupting her concentration, but she is clearly relieved to get to talk.

"No, it's only my third one! I'm so, so nervous! You're daughter sounds great in there and she didn't seem nervous at all. She must do a lot of these," she says.

"It's her first audition." I inform.

We continue to make small talk and I decide to share Ransford's great advice with the girl. I say, "You're in college for acting so I'm sure you've heard this before, but the best advice my daughter received was *just go in there and tell the story.*"

The minute I say it I wonder if in my kindness I've just accidentally betrayed my daughter. Maybe this wasn't the time or place to try and help anyone but my daughter. Damn it, it's hard to turn habits of sharing off. But maybe I should have.

The young woman, who again was just so nervous, says, "I've never heard that advice. That's great advice! Why don't they teach me that at college?"

We continue the small talk and then the girl, a perfect stranger 3 minutes before says, "I shouldn't think this, but the crazy thing is, I honestly hope your daughter gets the part. I shouldn't but I do. Because how cool would it be if she got the lead role on her first audition. That would be so great." She says it with total sincerity.

"That's so incredibly kind of you." I reply. Human beings can be awful, but they can also be so wonderful.

Then my attention goes back to the door.

Soon, Alyssa emerges.

Actually, she seems to burst.

And she's smiling.

Huge.

Thank you God.

She feels she nailed it.

As we head for the door, she's almost skipping. Her hair is somewhat bouncing. My heart's definitely dancing.

And she drops the script straight into the first trash can. Her acting teacher told her never keep an audition script. Throw it away so you have no temptation to wonder if you could have done any lines better.

Alyssa is a good student. She's teachable.

I'm so happy.

We exit and I say, "Can we take a photo in front of the building?" She's rarely in the mood for a picture with Dad anymore.

"Yes!" she says joyfully.

One the ride home, I find myself giving her a talk about what I've learned about following your dreams. I've made a living giving this talk for 22 years. But this talk is different. Same advice. Same lessons. But for the first time, I'm not a speaker or a coach. I'm something I've never been before.

I'm a dad sharing what he hopes his daughter to know about following her dreams.

She listens without saying a word.

She falls asleep.

I drive home the happiest father alive.

Oh, you are probably wondering if she got the part...
Yes, *she got the part!*

Hoboing Around

I arrived to her hospital bedside shortly after receiving the news from doctors that my mother was dying. My brother had prepared me for her condition, "Pat, she's pretty out of it. She's on a lot of pain meds so she only becomes conscious once in a while and only for a few sentences before she stops making sense. It's all the pain meds."

So I arrived expecting her recognition and tearful goodbyes, but little else.

Before I share what happened when I stepped into the hospital room, it's essential to understand something about my mother. She suffered a deeply broken childhood and it left her with emotional wounds of abandonment and abuse that would never really heal. It was like a heavy chain around her neck that would leave her feeling mostly unloved her entire life. Truth be told, it made life hard for her to live much of the time. She suffered severe depression throughout her adult life.

I was feeling afraid when I stepped into my mother's hospital room. Afraid I might feel too much. Afraid I might feel too little. Afraid I might be arriving too late. Afraid I might not be able to handle what I see. But as I stepped in, my fears were immediately quashed by the same enthusiastic greeting my mother has given me for 47 years, "Paaaaaatrick!" Followed by, "Miiiiiichael" She was propped up in the sitting position in the bed she was meant to die in. "Come here my sons!" There was no sign of a visitor named Death in her voice. I couldn't believe it. And inside, my heart spun a somersault into my throat and pushed tears into my eyes. She seemed 100% herself!

Quickly, I was hugging my mother, feeling the warmth of her face and arms, but through the hug I heard my mom exclaim, "Patrick, I've been hoboing around for days and I've had the most wonderful time!"

"Hoboing". It was a word I'd heard my mother say before in a way that could mean, wandering without a destination. But here, and now, it made no sense. My mother had been laying in a hospital bed for days. Then I remembered what my brother had said, "A few sentences before she stops making sense. It's all the pain meds." My heart began to sink. I wanted more time with my mother, my real mother.

But my mother couldn't contain herself to even let me get in words. She proceeded with urgency to tell us of the remarkable journey she'd just been on.

"Oh boys, I've just been wandering around like a hobo and it was the most wonderful thing! And boys I have been meeting the nicest people!"

Neither my brother nor I knew whether or not my mother was relating a dream to us or babbling. But she had more to tell us.

"And sons, they said they loved me! Can you believe it boys? They said they'd always loved me. Always!"

Now she was crying. "It was so wonderful! I told them I never wanted them to leave me, and boys, you'll never believe what they said! They said they never would! They'd be with me every day. And I asked them for how long? And they replied, 'Forever'".

Now she was crying the most profound joyful crying I've ever witnessed.

"I said to them, 'Forever, that's a long time!' and they answered, 'That's how it works here!'"

"Oh boys, they were very beautiful people, young. And they kept introducing me to more people that loved me! They were mystical. Oh sons, it was so beautiful! They loved me! Can you believe it? They loved me and they didn't even know me!"

It was my mother's deep crying while relating the experience that gave her words the deep emotional impact they had on me. I'd never seen my mother, let alone any human being, cry with as much joy and relief as I saw my mother cry throughout her story. She would tell us a few sentences and then cry out what seemed to be another decade of carried pain. Tell us more, and then cry more. Crying from the depths of her soul. Crying as if her lifetime of loneliness had been wiped clean. Crying as if she finally knew she was, always had been, and always would be loved.

After telling us her story, the conversation turned to us as a family. Our mother stayed propped up in her bed, 100% percent herself, talking and laughing and eye rolling with us as she always had, for the last sustained time, until late into the night. All words that wanted to be said between us were said. It would prove to be the last real day with her. It will be a day I forever think of as "the gift."

Nancy Combs, June 29, 1940 - June 17, 2014.
You Are Loved, Forever.

Thief!

One day in my mid-thirties, while my wife and I are living in downtown San Diego in a decent neighborhood, not a lot of crime, my wife looks out the window to our driveway and screams, "OMG, there is someone in our Jeep!"

I run to the window and I see what she sees, a man we don't know in our front seat apparently rummaging through the car!

I burst out of the house and yell, "Hey!" The man hears me and scrambles quickly out of the car and bursts into a full out sprint.

Suddenly I'm in cop movie, chasing a criminal down the street. Hurdling bushes, jumping cars, running down the middle of a road, chasing him for blocks. He's young and fast. But I'm keeping up!

I have no time to think about what I'm going to do if I catch up to him. I'm just running with the feeling that I have to catch this thief, this robber, this man who has been in my car. "Stop!" "Stop!!!" I yell.

And finally, I run him down. At first we're both just catching our breath. Then I say, "What did you take? What did you take?!"

He looks guilty. Perhaps even ashamed. "Money. I took money man!"

"Give me the money!" I say, and he hands over the few crumpled dollars and coins he found in my glove box.

"Why did you take my money?"

"I'm sorry man. I'm sorry." he says, now coming more clearly into my thoughts. He must be homeless. A young homeless guy. Some mother's lost son.

Still trying to catch my breath, I go, "You need money? Just ask. I'll help you out. Here's $20. Next time ask so that it's not stealing. Cool?"

The young man stares at me for a second, accepts the money and gives me a big hug. "Sorry."

So I walk back to my house. My wife greets me scared. "Oh my God! What happened? I was so afraid when you ran after him! What were you thinking? Did you catch him? Are you okay? What was he doing?!"

"Yes, yes I'm fine. I caught him. He was stealing money."

"What did you do?!" she asked.

"I gave him $20. And told him to ask next time. We parted friends."

My wife says, "You did what!?!?!!?!?"

I said, "Honey, he obviously needed help."

We still laugh about that day.

What if your goal in life was above money, above right and wrong, and centered on adding love to people's lives? In your business and in your personal life? A heart centered approach to life connects and adds love.

Love is what life is really all about.

Hells Halsy

First I noticed I couldn't eat well. Couldn't quite chew the same way. It was difficult, and rice milk from my cold cereal kept dripping out of my mouth. My, what a sloppy eater I'm being this morning, I thought and kept on reading Steve Martin's autobiography.

Next, my left eye started burning. Apparently my contact lens had something underneath it. "I'm off to a terrible start this morning. I need to hit the reset button and start this day over," I thought as I headed back upstairs to my bathroom.

I took out my contacts and jumped back in the shower. I figured a shower would moisten my eye and wake my mouth up. After the shower, my left eye just refused to accept the contact lens I was trying to put over it. And then, looking into the mirror, I suddenly realized why. I could no longer blink my left eye.

For a second I was intrigued, but then I had a horrible suspicion something was wrong with my whole face. I tried to smile into the mirror and realized the entire left side of my face was completely unresponsive. Intrigue turned to alarm. Oh shit!

I googled.

"Stroke is the fifth leading cause of death in the U.S.

"Every 4 minutes someone dies from stroke.

"A stroke is a 'brain attack'. It can happen to anyone at any time. It occurs when blood flow to an area of brain is cut off. When this happens, brain cells are deprived of oxygen and begin to die. When brain cells die during a stroke, abilities controlled by that area of the brain such as memory and muscle control are lost.

"People who have larger strokes may be permanently paralyzed on one side of their body or lose their ability to speak.

"A stroke is a medical emergency, and treatment must be sought as quickly as possible."

I called my wife, who was out on errands. I spoke calmly but with urgency. "Honey, you better come home. I'm pretty sure I've had a stroke. And the internet says I better call 911 right away—that it could save my life."

My wife came within a semester of becoming a Naturopathic Doctor. She first tried to argue my conclusion. "There's no way you had a stroke! You're healthy. You've eaten vegan for 15 years. You don't eat animal fat. Or much sugar. There's NO way you've had a stroke. It just doesn't make sense."

"Okay honey, but tell that to the left-side of my face which is completely dead to me," I replied with a calm that surprised me.

"I'm coming home to take you to the emergency room," she said as I heard her car engine racing.

A lot of people on my mother's side of my family have had strokes. I have it in my head that strokes are often precursors to heart attacks which can strike shortly after the stroke. I sat at our kitchen counter steeped in a feeling that I could very well be living the last moments of my life, and I was oddly at peace.

I grabbed for pen and paper and began writing what

I loved about my life the most. I hoped to capture this moment of extraordinary clarity.

Love. Given and received.

Surprises.

Moments when dreams came true.

Laughs.

Spiritual miracles.

Children, especially your own.

Making love.

Creativity.

And dedicating yourself to something you feel matters.

I heard our car racing up our street faster than ever before, and I concluded my reflection on life with "How much times does each of us have left to experience these wonders of life?"

I was completely at peace as my wife drove us at high speed to the hospital. I noticed beautiful flowers on the side of the road. I felt good that I was properly insured for death or disability. I had done well in my responsibility to ensure my wife and daughter would be okay no matter what happened to me. And I had lived very well.

All the stress was falling on my wife, and likely my daughter—who from the back seat made me pinky promise I wasn't faking that the left-side of my face didn't work.

My wife likely didn't notice that music she doesn't like was playing in the car, Cheap Trick—that's how far away her mind was. She kept insisting that it made no sense that I would have a stroke, not with my animal free diet, non-smoking habits, young age, and exercise regimen.

But there it was staring back at her—my face was

no longer working. I was slurring. I could see her true concern and I found it sweet.

"You didn't have a stroke. You have Bell's palsy," the emergency room Dr. informed me.

Bell's palsy is a disorder of the facial nerve, or cranial nerve VII. Something mysterious happens to this nerve—they really don't know what yet—and it can cause complete paralysis of half your facial muscles.

Around 30,000-40,000 Americans get it every year. Turns out almost everyone you talk to will tell you that they know someone who had it—everyone except my wife and me. My wife's father had even had it, but she didn't know until she told him about me.

The emergency room doctor told me it was a temporary, couple month condition for about 80% of people. "So you're telling me there's a 1 in 5 chance only half my face will work for the rest of my life," I half-jokingly said back.

He gave me steroids and anti-virals in a small paper cup to take before I left. But I didn't take them. When he wasn't looking, I threw them in the trash.

I'm skeptical of big pharma and pills doled out like candy. I like alternative medicine and energy healings. And my wife whispered in my ear, "You don't need those. I googled and you need Vitamin B-12 shots. Skip those pills."

So into the trash they went, along with my 80% chance of recovery, probably. My wife smiled approvingly. I felt smart, not stupid.

I'm sure Bell's palsy would be inconvenient at any time in one's life, but my Bell's palsy showed up five days before I was set to depart on the biggest tour of my comedy career, a 15 city tour through the Carolinas for my show 'Man 1, Bank 0'.

Whether or not to do this comedy tour was now seriously in question. Bell's palsy is even less sexy looking than Chicken Pox. At least Chicken Pox allows you to blink and talk normal. With Bell's palsy I looked and talked like a drunken, ugly pirate. Or Mad-Eye Mooney in Harry Potter. My left eye, open extra-wide, red with irritation - always watching. My speech was slurred and I was unable to pronounce "F's" "P's" or "B's".

Ironically Bell's palsy was among the most impossible things for me to pronounce. It sounded like "I have Hells Halsy". If I dropped the F-bomb while looking at myself in the mirror it sounded like "Huck." If I introduced myself, my name was "Hatrick." Talking and explaining my condition to people was very hucked up.

When I woke up the next day I took enough vitamins and supplements to fill a suitcase. I lined up a full day schedule of acupuncture, massage, and chiropractic care that I hoped would get the left-side of my face to come back from vacation before my comedy tour. And I began giving myself twice-daily injections of Vitamin B-12 in the butt, not easy at first—as I'm afraid of needles. "If Rambo could stitch up his own wounds, I can do this," I'd think before closing my eyes and sticking myself in the ass.

It was all exhausting. My eye was irritated from being open too much. I was still learning to manually blink it. It was either tape my eye completely shut, wear an eye patch and go full-pirate, or reach up every sixty seconds and pull my eye lid down for a few seconds manually.

I was not ready to go full Black Beard yet. Even the massage was tiring as my massage therapist, Ted, treated my condition as if it were something you rooted out with an elbow crushed all the way to the bones. "Ted, you're trying to relax my face not get me to give up government secrets, buddy."

I hoped it would all help rapidly as my tour was just days away. But it didn't help a bit. I actually looked worse and worse. The right side of my face was taking over, pulling the left side of my face its way, because I didn't look bad enough with the crazy eye, slack face and drool.

I'd lived with half-a-face for four days. And although I had slurred speech, the most limiting thing was my inability to give others a nice smile. They say you're only half dressed without a smile. I felt only half-dressed as I interacted with others. I'd try smiling to people I passed by, and people wouldn't smile back at me as usual. I knew I looked bad but what I missed the most was my smile.

It was time to tour or cancel. I walked to the mirror and did everything in my power to move the left side of my face. Nothing. Not an inch. It was stark.

I felt entirely the same on the inside, but couldn't move the left-side of my face even a smidgen. I reached up and pulled my eye shut for a manual blink. Then applied a piece of tape to keep it shut through the night while I slept. I was a freak show. But I was going to go on tour in the morning. I worried it might be among the worst decisions of my career.

My good friend David was traveling with me. He'd often go on tour with me to help out and keep me company. This time, I knew I couldn't do it without his support.

We met at an airport in North Carolina and as we drove to my first show, our conversation stayed lightly on the crazy story of my catastrophe. But when we pulled into the parking lot of the theatre that displayed my show poster, fear and doubt filled my being.

"David, there are 300 people in that theatre that paid to see comedy. You see me. Don't let me go in there if I'm making a mistake. I'd rather cancel at the last minute than go down in flames. Be honest with me, do you think I can pull this off with only half-a-face?"

David stared at me and assessed the situation. His face was dead serious.

"Bro, I will be nothing but honest with you. Not just because you're my best friend, but also because factually, I've seen your show more than any other person in the world and I know the demands of what you do. I also know that your face is your primary instrument when you're up there on stage. You use it to not only tell the story and deliver the punch lines, but often in the show, you makes faces that are key to the scene. I know the scenes where you make people laugh just by changing your face to a specific expression. So I get it," he assessed.

"Okay Dave, so what's your bottom line? Yay or Nay, bro?"

"Hold on a sec Patrick. I also want to say that when you were telling me by phone you had Bell's palsy and that half your face wasn't working, I believed you. But until you got in this car and I saw you—I had *No* idea how bad it was. Until you see it, you can't really believe it," Dave said.

"Yikes, so cancel?"

"Hold on bro. I'm going to be honest with you. You look terrible. And you talk like a drunk."

"So I need to cancel," I said wanting Dave to put an end to my ever increasing anxiety.

"Hold up bro..!" Dave continued. "With all that said, if it were anyone else I'd tell them to cancel. *But you're not anyone else* and your show is not just a bunch of jokes strung together. I think between the strength of the story you're telling in your show, the slides you're using, the props you so brilliantly employ, and your personality—I think you can pull it off Patrick. That's my honest opinion."

"I was hoping you'd say cancel, Dave."

"Don't cancel bro. You can do this. Go give it a try. Hell, we're in a small town in North Carolina, who cares if you fail here. And if you tank, you can cancel the rest of the tour. But you came 3,000 miles. Go in there and give it a try. We both know how hard you worked to get to here in your theatre career. Just remember to carry a napkin on stage for your drool. That shit's nasty!" he concluded laughing.

I made a plan for how to open my show that night.

I walked out on stage and did my opening joke as usual, no deviation. It was obvious to the audience that I had a severe speech slur but the joke got a laugh anyway. Then according to plan, I talked about the elephant in the room.

"You robably noticed I have a severe slur. I'm happy to hell you that I hidn't have a stroke. I have a condition called hells halsey. Many of you have heard of it. It's a hemporary condition where half your hace goes on vacation hor a hew months. The hood news is heople on hhis side of the heatre (pointing to my right) will hardly notice. But you guys (pointing to my left) are screwed."

The line got a big laugh and the rest of the show went more than alright. It was a hard performance for sure, tough because throughout the show my mind waged a battle with all the slurring and difficult pronunciation.

I bit my tongue many times. I wiped drool and I had to remember to keep manually blinking my eye between show bits. But when it was all said and done and the curtain came down, half the audience gave me a standing ovation—which was perfect all things considered. I was going to be okay!

The next night I wore sunglasses to lessen people's exposure to what Dave and I nicknamed my Zombie eye, always watching, always vigilant.

Back home, I kept up my regimen of supplements, massage, and alternative healthcare. My face was not improving but I noticed my brain was evolving a way to work around the difficult words that began with "F", "B" and "P." My brain began playing Taboo with these three letters. If I was about to say, "We have a fence around our pool", my brain would quickly reroute the sentence to "We have a chain link barrier."

It slowed down my ability to speak, but I found it fascinating and marvelous that the brain would do such a thing.

A month later, there was no sign of any improvement. I had gotten to a nice place where I often forgot I had Bell's palsy, although I maintained my daily regimen of health activities that I hoped would woo the left side of my face into returning to duty.

I gave shows and inspirational speeches with the right-side of my face doing all the work. It was always a conversation on planes with strangers. Most people knew someone that had had it. One woman confessed that she thought I was blind in one eye. She then asked me why it's called Bell's palsy. I told her it's named after the first person to diagnose it. And then I mused that it should have been named something more descriptive such as "Two face" or "Lazy face."

The ongoing effect, that was the hardest, was that my having "Coma face" made it harder for people to connect with me. I lost half my smile and it was easily apparent to me that many people would avoid looking at me without even knowing they were doing so.

At first it made me feel broken, but that passed and I learned to smile more with my eyes. I also began to put more effort into saying things to people that would put a smile on their face quickly. I came to a point of being entirely comfortable with myself.

At worst it felt like I was speaking to people through a mask. But mostly, I just felt like I was myself and had to work a little harder to put people around me at ease. This was a beautiful gift.

In late May, almost four months into having Bell's palsy, I returned to see a doctor about it. He had seen many cases of it. He informed me that unfortunately, my Bell's palsy was almost certainly a permanent condition. I was the 1 in 5. I probably should have taken those first pills.

I left his office deep in thought and I arrived home and went straight to my mirror. Yes, I saw Mad Eye Mooney staring back at me, but only for a second.

Then I saw my real self, me behind my face. I saw my joyful spirit, I saw my peaceful essence. I saw my kind heart. I saw my gifts and talents that could uplift others with inspiration and laughter. I saw a perfect smile in my eyes. And a phrase someone had said to me 20 years before came rushing into my mind.

Handsome is as handsome does.

It finally really meant something to me. Being attractive isn't about reflecting good looks—it's about radiating goodness.

I still felt like myself. I still made people laugh in my comedy shows. I still inspired people from the stage. I still made friends wherever I went. I'd learned to smile more with my eyes. I used more humor to break down the fear that some had of my face—that looked on one side like dripping wax. My broken looks were permanent, but I was going to be just fine.

Two months later, my left-face came sauntering in from its 6 month vacation, refreshed and willing to resume its duties, without so much as an apology, explanation, or T-shirt from the gift shop.

Nonetheless, I was happy to have it back.

If you look carefully at me on certain days—especially if I'm a little extra tired—you can however still see my left-face being a little extra relaxed, seemingly saying, "If you don't get more rest, I'm outta here for the Bahamas again."

Life Reflections

—What Bells Palsey Taught Me - 02/23/2008

The greatest thing about life is the love you give and receive.

> The moments when you loved someone so well
> they smiled a deep and peaceful joy.
> The moments when someone loved you so well
> you felt seen and magnificent.

> The greatest thing about life is the surprises.
> The thrilling opportunity you receive out of the blue.
> The perfect words you needed that happened to
> be written on the wall you happened upon.
> The song that perfectly matches your situation
> while it's happening.

> The greatest thing about life is that it actually
> affords you 'dream come true' moments, charging
> you a reasonable entrance fee of only risk and
> persistence and belief.

> The greatest thing about life is the laughs.
> The laughs that emerged out of nowhere.
> The laughs that were created by a friend.
> The laughs you prompted in someone else.
> Laughter is both a magnificent feeling and a
> great sound.

> The great thing about life is the miracles.

The spiritual ones that suddenly remind you
that the most amazing reality is the unseen
reality playing a part in everything we do.
The miracles that remind us that we are
spiritual beings. That the universe is very loving.
Especially the miracles that feel like a giant
hug from God.

The greatest thing about life is children.
Especially your children. They are as close
to God as I have ever come.

The greatest thing about life is making love.
Not sex. But love. The kind where you intertwine
in energy that feels like silk and magic. The kind
that heals you.

The greatest thing about life is creativity.
Creativity and sex are sisters—both very
passionate and exuberant feelings. Pinnacle
experiences.

The greatest thing about life is dedicating yourself
to something you passionately feel matters.
For a long time. No matter what the odds or what
others think. As long as it engrosses you and makes
you come alive.

How much time does each of us have left
to experience these wonders of life?

Love, P

Angry Jedi

My hip hurts today and as I was dropping off my kids at school I started thinking about sex and old age—these are the signs of middle age. In middle age, if you have kids, most of your life is about driving your kids and doing for your kids, and there are increasing signs that old age is stalking you.

For my son's birthday we had a gigantic, humungous, inflatable obstacle course placed right smack onto our driveway. It looked like a yellow, red, and blue cruise ship docked at our home. The driveway being 40 feet, the inflatable oceanliner being 50 feet, so the last 10 feet hung out into the street and made for a more exciting exit into traffic. Sure, inflated walls are a good obstacle, but dodging cars, now that's a challenge for six year olds.

It was a Star Wars themed birthday party and at some point I made an entrance dressed as Darth Vader and gave each six year old boy a chance to duel me in a light-saber battle.

Listen to me carefully: *Never* give six year old boys light sabers and permission to strike at you in a 'duel' because it turns out that six year old boys apparently have A LOT OF PENT UP ANGER.

From behind my Darth Vader mask, which maintained an even temperature inside of 150 degrees, all I could see was six year old boys swinging with both arms as hard as they humanly could... Which turns out to be pretty damned hard!

All the parents thought I was playfully fighting back, but between the suit heat which was like a session of hot-yoga, and the boys who were swinging at me like Derek Jeter, I was actually fighting hard to reduce the amount of bruises I'd have the next day.

I would fall down to try and signal the end of the fight, but then a dad, (Grant) yells out "Finish him off!" Well that earned me another 10 clubbings. Then all the parents apparently got bored watching young Jedi beat a grown man with batons, and left.

And when they were gone the boys decided to all attack Darth Vader together at once. It was ugly. I was curled up in the fetal position with six youth wailing on me with light sabers, similar to a YouTube video of police wailing on a person for protesting.

Happy Birthday Son, can the beating stop now?!

Where was I? Oh yes, my hip hurts because I was playing on the inflatable a lot. Felt like a kid on that thing. Need more play in my life like that, where I'm just running and sliding and chasing and laughing because most of my life is just boring by comparison.

I came home from my comedy tour to a small mountain of mail that was full of bills, and the endless paperwork required these days of small business owners; they sure know how to take the fun out it.

So about my hip hurting. Yesterday I had a conversation with a friend about her 91 year old neighbor who talks to her about getting old. At 91 she's the same mentally as a she ever was but her body won't allow the things she used to enjoy doing and the things she took for granted. Like walking.

It really got me thinking about how damn lucky I am right now. I'm 48, everything in my body works super perfect, anything is physically possible for me. Walking, running, yoga, surfing, jumping, obstacle courses, dodging traffic, and sex.

But for how long? For how much longer? When comes the day when I wake up and can't walk without my hip hurting because it doesn't work anymore? When comes the day I can't chase a kid on an obstacle course or take a beating from 6 armed and aggressive six year olds? When comes the day I can't enjoy sex without breaking or dislocating something?

If I play hard on an inflatable football-field-sized obstacle course, yes my hip hurts the following day. But I'm lucky because everything on my body works and I can still do it all, so I want to really appreciate my health and take advantage of it. I want to appreciate that this hurt in my hip is a whisper from my body that says, "Someday you won't have all this great health, so get out and use me to have as much fun as you can while all your parts still work. You're young now, but not forever."

I want to age gracefully and part of that graceful aging is deep appreciation for all the good your body still offers. I'm glad to have this home that can still run obstacle courses and take beat downs from young Jedi. It won't last forever.

Hearts Talk

My wife and I were laying on opposite sides of the bed with our backs toward one another. Relationships aren't always easy and we were going through a hard time. We'd been sleeping this way for a week.

I wasn't proud of it but I also didn't know what to do. We both had too much 'I'm right and you're wrong'. So there we were with enough space between us in bed for a walkway. Love can be devastatingly hard.

I had no plans to bridge the gap between us but suddenly I was a filled with an unexpected prompting.

Out of nowhere I had a strong prompt that seemed to be nudging me to pull Deanna close to me, face to face and hold her. This thought really caught me by surprise because I was stubborn and had zero intention of doing anything this morning to unfreeze the cold between us.

Pulling my wife close didn't seem like my thought, nor did it seem like *a thought*. It just felt like a prompt I was supposed to follow. I rolled toward Deanna, fully knowing this was going to come as a surprise to her, and also expecting my advance could be met with a strong rebuff. She was hurt too.

To my surprise she let me roll her over and pull her close. Even getting to this closeness made me grateful because the distance between us was killing me.

Then I felt it. An unmistakable beam of energy flowing back and forth between our two hearts. "Do you feel that?!" I asked her.

"What? Feel what?" she replied. She did not feel it, but I could as plain as day. And I could see it in my mind—it looked like the photon energy they used to beam up the crew on Star Trek. It was as wide as the lid of a jar. And it was connecting our two hearts.

"Don't move an inch!" I whispered, "Something amazing is happening between our hearts. An energetic connection of some kind. I can see it and feel it, in my mind. Don't move!" My wife laid silently without moving. And tears streamed down her face.

It lasted about 5 minutes. It was entirely real to me. I don't really know what it was. My guess is that hearts have an energetic way of synching up; that our hearts had gotten out of synch and that the prompting I received was a means to get our hearts resynchronized.

Sometimes the phrase that pops into my mind when I think about this mystical experience is simply, "Hearts Talk." Now I believe they do.

Author William Bruce Cameron said, "Not everything that can be counted counts, and not everything that counts can be counted."

Laying together in the middle of our bed, my wife and I both apologized to one another, expressed our love, and returned to the closeness we both desired. I was in awe of the magical things that are on a different spectrum than our ordinary senses.

Dunkin Donuts

My mother died about two years ago. And my brother and I were both there for the final days.

So my brother is a Dunkin Donuts guy. Me, Starbucks. It tells you a lot about us. Me, I'm stupid enough to believe you can't get a good coffee at Dunkin Donuts. My brother doesn't want a "latte with soy milk" or to pay an absurd $5 for it. I've never wandered into a Dunkin Donuts. He wouldn't waste his money at a Starbucks. Never has. Never would.

So there came this moment near to my mom's death, when I had to say goodbye. For the last time. I had been at her side, sleeping in her hospital room for about two weeks. But now she was unconscious, heavily medicated and would not be coming back. I was leaving her, having been told by the head nurse I needed to go now so my mother would let go.

So came the time for my final moments with my mother.

My brother said he would give me all the time I needed alone with her, "Call me or text me when you want to be picked up. Take all the time you need little brother."

It was evening. And silent when I walked in her

room. My mother was still there, sleeping under blankets. Hooked up to IVs or some shit.

She was asleep like the dead.

At night this wing of the hospital is a ghost town.

It's dark in her room.

I walk to my mother's side. This is the woman who birthed me. Her hair is gray. The skin on her arms still looks young, but hangs loose from age. I know her face so well.

This is the blood of my blood.

I take her hand. And hold it inside of mine. It is warm. How odd that it's smaller than my hand. When I was a child it felt so big.

This is the woman who took me to the park to feed the ducks.

This is the woman who gave me a home, even when she couldn't afford it.

This is the woman who played with me and made me laugh.

This is the woman who got me a graduation present by trading away her washer and dryer.

This is the woman who fed me. Who cooked for me. Who taught me. Who worked nights for me. Who praised me. Who always answered every single call from me with unimaginable enthusiasm.

This is the woman who gave every thing she had for me. Everything.

I want to crumble...

I don't know how to do this.

"Mom, I want to thank you for so much.

"For feeding me, for raising me, for always being there for me.

"For loving me always.

"For keeping a roof over our heads

"For all the times you tucked me in as a child for coming to all my track meets.

"For getting me to go to college.

"Mom, *I love you.*

"And I realize I can't actually thank you enough. There's too much. But thank you for being such a good mother. Thank you my sweet mother.

"I will miss you so, so, so much. And I don't know how to do this.

"How to say goodbye to you.

"But I love you. And I will see you again my mother.

"Good by my sweet mother."

And then I kiss her on the forehead. I take a deep breath of her in.

And next, I must find a way to stand up and walk out on my mother. For the last time ever. I don't know if I can do it. I didn't know you had to do things this hard in life.

This is real. It is permanent. It cannot be undone. It is an end. It is a disappearance.

I squeeze my beautiful mom's hand. Pull up her blanket.

And walk out.

I make it down the empty hall. Down the elevator. Before I collapse onto the chair in the empty lobby sobbing.

It is done.

I have seen my mother for the last time. And said my goodbyes. And realized you can't thank a parent for all they do. They do too much to put to words.

I text my brother

PATRICK COMBS: "Come get me."

MIKE COMBS: "I'm outside in the parking lot."

I walk out to my older brother.

79

He has a look of deep compassion in his eyes.
And a Starbucks in his hand.
"Here little brother, let's go for a drive."

Morgan Freeman

Some stories I've kept for only family and friends. This was one of them. And I assure you from the bottom of my heart it's the truth. Heck, if I were changing the story it wouldn't be Morgan Freeman, that's for damn sure.

It started in Brain Training. My friend Beejal had opened a Brain Training practice in our town of Encinitas. It was cutting edge technology. You went in, they hooked your head up to the most sophisticated brain wave mapping technology in the world, and a brain wave practitioner in a lab coat put you through a series of exercises that trained you to consciously alter your own brain wave states. Science fiction in real life.

I didn't know how much stake to put in such a thing, but it struck me that there'd be no harm in being among the first to really give it a go. I told Beejal I wanted to come twice a week for an entire month.

I'd go in and sit in a big, comfortable, reclining chair. My head would be covered carefully with what I'd call "diodes and wires", and then when they flipped the switch, in front of me on several large computer monitors, I'd see my brain waves reflected back at me in color. There was no sign of any real intelligence...but whatever.

I quickly got over my skepticism when I began to

see an undoubtable correlation between the exercises they were having me do and the changing patterns of my brain waves. When I did an exercise for focus, my Beta waves went up. When I did a relaxation exercise, my Alpha waves rose. It all became very straight forward. It was sound science and I looked forward to my sessions in the chair.

I was particularly excited about one discovery. When I'd smile ear to ear like a mad man, my brain waves lit up in a way that elevated my entire brain function. Even the white-coated, licensed practitioners were excited to see the effect. Apparently no one else had smiled so much in the chair.

Three weeks into this, the brain wave trainer gave me a simple exercise for relaxation. I was to close my eyes and imagine I was on a beach, and blow my worries and troubles into balloons, and watch them float away.

No problem, I closed my eyes and began.

It was easy to picture myself on the beach since I live in a beach town. And it was easy to pick a worry and imagine that I was blowing it into a red, green, yellow, or blue balloon. Then I'd imagine tying off the balloon and watch it rise up and over the blue waters of the Pacific Ocean.

But the visualization gave me concerns. Where were these balloons going to land? Were birds going to choke on them? Were they going to be garbage in the sea?

And then it happened.

My imagining myself on the beach was replaced with me *being* on the beach. Let me say that again to be clear. Suddenly, I somehow went from being in a chair *picturing* myself on the beach, to *standing* on a beach. And standing on the beach for me was as real as wherever you are right now as you read this story.

I told you I kept this story for only family and friends.

Now, there's one other detail that matters. I was suddenly standing on the beach *with* Morgan Freeman, who was dressed in a white suit. And if you're thinking, that sounds like Morgan Freeman playing the role of God in the movie *Bruce Almighty* with Jim Carrey, we're on the same page.

I was on a real beach and I was aware that Morgan Freeman felt entirely like "God". His presence was so loving.

Now, *this* was *not* in accord with my spiritual philosophy! I like my God as a brilliant loving light and a loving presence in all of us. I like to refer to my God as "Universe"; I've *never* subscribed to God as a Person, in the sky or on the ground.

My first thought about this extraordinary situation was, "Come on! Morgan Freeman?! Anyone but Morgan Freeman! No one's going to believe me. I won't be able to tell anyone about this." And then he spoke.

"But it works for you, right?"

He had me there. It did. Completely. I thought Morgan Freeman was the perfect guy to play God in *Bruce Almighty*.

"Yes, it does," I replied.

"So you're worried about the balloons landing in the ocean?" he asked.

"I am," I said almost embarrassed that he could read my thoughts.

"I'll tell you what. You blow your troubles into another balloon and I'll take care of the where the balloon goes. How does that sound?" he asked me in his unmistakable voice.

It was an agreeable idea to me so I blew up another

balloon and released it over the ocean. But again, I worried about where it would land.

He smiled at me in a way that looked like he was holding back a laugh. "How about this?" he said snapping his fingers. "Is this better?"

When he snapped his fingers we were both suddenly in a meadow with no ocean in sight. It was a warmer place with perfectly still air. I smelled the grass. I saw the trees. I heard the silence of nature. And I knew how amazing this was. But any sense of awe that I had was background to an absolutely incredible feeling of being loved that I had been experiencing since whomever this was showed up as Morgan Freeman. I want to say God to be honest, but I don't know any more than what I'm telling here. I felt like I was talking to God, but I was looking at Morgan Freeman.

"I feel so loved by you," I said next in the middle of the meadow.

"That's because you are," Morgan replied.

"Really? Wow, I feel it. It's amazing," I said.

"You're amazing," he said back.

"Do you want to try blowing up another balloon?" he asked me.

"Not really. I'm just happy being here with you... This meadow is gorgeous," I remarked.

"Thanks," he said without any hint of irony. But I laughed. He in return just smiled and gave his head a small wag. The head motion that to me says, It's true.

The love I was feeling in every cell of my body was sheer magnificence.

"You really love me?" I asked.

"Entirely. And nothing less," he answered.

"I feel it! Can I ask you a question?" I ventured.

"Sure," he answered.

"Why are you here with me?"

"I'm always here with you."

"Hmmm..." I said as I thought about his reply. "It's wonderful. You just feel like a friend. A friend who *Really* loves me."

He smiled at me, looking perfectly amazing in his white suit and white tie. "I hope we're friends! I love watching you." he said.

"You do?" I asked feeling shy.

"Of course. Also, you were worried about the balloons. I came here to help you not worry. Don't worry so much. You've got nothing to worry about," he said.

I felt amazing. I felt extraordinarily amazing. Perfectly safe. Perfectly loved. And totally liked.

"I would just stand here forever with you."

Morgan smiled.

"How'd it go?" interrupted my brainwave technician.

It was over. I was back in the chair.

"Good," I said. "*Really* good... I had a little trouble worrying about where the imaginary balloons would land but I got over it."

"Good, good," she said.

I asked to see the recording of my brainwave patterns during the exercise. She brought them up on screen.

"Oh, you went deep this time! You went into Theta and even some Delta. Delta brain wave rhythms are associated with advanced meditation practices. I'd say you got very relaxed," she said.

"Yeah, I think I went deep on that one," I said. I wasn't about to tell her it seemed like I spoke to God and he looked like Morgan Freeman.

I told my five year old son that a monkey was sent into space. I said, "Son can you imagine what that monkey was thinking?!" My son says, "Yay! All the bananas for me!"

When my son was four years old, he saw our neighbor's house completely tented in yellow and blue stripes for fumigation. He asked, "Dad why do you think they covered that house?"

Me: "Why do *you* think they covered it son?"

Will: "Maybe for 3 reasons... Maybe because they don't want spiders and bugs to get inside. OR, because they're having a birthday party and want to have it at night. OR, because they're having a parade and don't want us to see!"

Never just answer your kids' questions. First get their guesses.

me dad because I want my son to grow up with a deep knowingness that he had one. And I hope our playing hockey helps him be popular with the ladies.

This morning my son was cracking me up with a word mistake.

So... my son really wants to climb a wall with me using a grappling hook and rope, like I did when I was kid.

But because he's four, this morning he's getting the word wrong as I drive him to school.

"Dad, can we get a hooker?"

"Dad, I want to get a hooker and play with a hooker."

"Dad, are hookers a lot of money?"

"Uhm son, it's a hook. Very important. HOOK. You can't go to school until you get the word right. Hook son! Hook!"

I hope to burst as a SuperNova. I want to explode into a million creations, to add beautiful hues to the color of the universe.

What's bursting inside of you?

Love, Patrick

Total Shite

Tonight's show was absolute *Shite*. Total shite. Complete shite. God you have to love theatre because it's live, not Memorex as they say, and it can go really totally wrong.

I'm touring the U.K. for the first time with my show Man 1, Bank 0. It's going really well. Last night was a flawless show in a gorgeous art deco, 500 seat theatre, - which we sold out—and our stage set looked fantastic. My crew didn't miss a single light or sound cue, and my performance earned a standing ovation. In other words, the evening lived up to the hype.

Tonight we drove a surprisingly long, long, long way out of town. I can testify that the U.K. has a LOT of countryside. Hours later, we arrive at this really amazing quaint, and incredibly scenic little village (I'm exaggerating when I say village because it's really just a few beautiful cottages set on a lush green hillside. This is the place you want to go for a romantic get-away with your loved one in the far, far, far, far old-country of green, green grass and fields, staying in a vine covered brick cottage and only leaving your place and taking a break from fireside-side sex to have a little hike through the gorgeous countryside. Or possibly to mosey down to the Town Hall, slash restaurant, directly adjacent to the field of sheep, to see a show—me being tonight's show...

My posters are tacked, dotting fence posts along the lane, right next to laminated flyers that have a photo of an older gentlemen wearing a vest and an ascot, pointing his finger towards you with the words, "Your Village Hall Needs You—relax and NATTER with friends and discuss our issues." The Threlkeld Activities Association.

Anyway, my stage director, manager, and myself arrive at the venue ready to set up the stage and lights with the help their crew.

So the first thing is—it's not a theatre! It's just a hall. My manager Francis, a consummate professional and one of Ireland's top promoters, is shocked and apologetic immediately. "I'm sorry Patrick, nobody told me. Lots of great acts come here to perform, I was told."

Secondly, there is *No stage*. At the discovery of this, Francis just looks at me, raises his eyebrows, and shrugs his shoulders a bit. He looks frightened.

We build a make-shift stage out of platforms. It looks like total crap. Also missing is a "dressing room" where I can prepare for my performance. It is decided that since I do need a backstage area to get ready, to change into my show costume, to enter the stage from— one will have to be created using one roll-able wall. A wall so small only one metal folding chair can be hidden behind it. This two foot area is where I will need to "hide" once we open the doors for the audience. It is from here I will enter the stage—it is a one step up and one step forward journey from this dressing room to center stage.

I am pining for last night's venue.

Next, it's time to "set the lights". This is an hour's long endeavor where the theater's stage hands get up on ladders, aim a multitude of lights at various zones on my stage. Lighting is an enormously important role in any successful show—usually. But tonight, Francis can't even look at me when the stage lights, all five of them, are carried in by a woman who drove them here in her car...

Cathal is my stage manager. He travels with us as an integral part to the success of every show. And I'm lucky to have him. He's a 78 year old theater legend. He has performed, directed, and produced some of the finest plays in the finest venues in the world. He says to the young woman who is running tonight's venue, half-jokingly, "This is the low point of my career. I used to manage lowly musicians in bad night clubs, but it's been all downhill since then."

We're as ready as we'll ever be to open the doors for the audience. 100 metal chairs are ready to receive them. Francis has come to my 2 foot backstage chair and said, "Break a leg and just try and survive."

Our audience tops out at 18 old people. I'll let you in on something you learn when you do comedy professionally—only 18 people in sea of 82 empty chairs is a good reason to drink before you go onstage, because laughs are going to be few and far between. Throw on top of that an ugly make-shift stage, no theatrical lighting, and the actor entering stage from behind a roll-able wall—and everyone in attendance is questioning their choice to attend, including myself.

After the most embarrassing entrance I've ever made onto a stage—the two step journey from behind my little wall—I begin the show. And in no time, I realize the few lights we did set to light scenes are completely going wrong. I move stage left and the lights turn on stage RIGHT, so I'm performing in the dark. I move center stage and the lights are on stage right. Just as I'm feeling that I can't survive this—the first sound cue comes in 10 seconds late. And for the rest of the night, I am performing with random light cues and random sound cues. 18 people look mostly confused. They are trying to make sense out of it all, why the sound of fax machine rings out in the dark, during a scene that I am supposedly walking outside in mid-afternoon.

By intermission, I'm sitting in my "chair behind the wall" and I'm dreading another 45 minutes of show to perform. It's amazing really that performance can be the highest high or the lowest low. You've never felt so bad as when you are the only person dying on a stage for 90 minutes. When a show is tanking, it's the longest 90 minutes of your life, I promise you. Every line out of your mouth feels like labor. You are doing your lines while wishing for "Someone pull the fire alarm". You look out and see people who look as unhappy as you feel yourself. Show biz, when it's not working is excruciating.

Francis pokes his head in at intermission and says, "Are you okay? Is there anything I can get you?" I reply, "Four pints and a shot please."

Anyhow, the show ends, the audience claps lots, and I feel like it was the worst show of my life. Then we pack up as quick as possible and head for pints in town.

The more we drink, the more we laugh. Cathal says, "Patrick, you need to fire your light technician and your sound man... I'm so sorry Patrick, whenever you were stage right, I lit stage left. I blew the lighting cues as bad as humanly possible."

Francis adds, "I was trying to do the sound cues but the controls were in a cabinet. To reach them, I had to stick my head into it with a flashlight to try and see what I was doing every time and I missed every cue."

We almost laughed ourselves off the barstools reliving every mistake.

At the very end of the pub drinking, Cathal says to me, "I don't know what your philosophy is Patrick, but you're a joy to tour with because it's amazing how you handle nights like this. Any other performer would be yelling at the top of their lungs at how shite the lights and sound were but not you."

All the mistakes made me feel like a B-List hack, but my philosophy is simple: What's to get upset about really? *Nothing.* I'm on tour with two great guys, men I truly call friends. And as long as we're all willing to have a laugh about it, it will go down in our memories as a great time. It's just theatre not life-saving surgery. And you can't really know the highs, if you don't have the lows.

Anyway, we drank in the pub till 2 a.m. and laughed enough to more than compensate for the 18 people who didn't. As we're getting up to go, Cathal says with the utmost sincerity, "I've directed and seen shows for 50 years, Patrick, and your show is so good it can play anywhere in the world. But may I recommend you never put tonight's show on your resume."

We'll need some sleep because there's another show tomorrow. The three of us stumble out of the pub into the night. Francis says, "Follow me, I'll be right behind you!"

Only in Mexico

At the beginning of this summer, my friend Tim and I drove into Baja, Mexico for a couple days of vacation. Tim's a paraglider, so we were headed for the renowned cliffs of Las Salinas.

On the drive down I told Tim about my dream car, a 1983 convertible Cadillac Biarritz. Red. I'd seen one for the first time recently while vacationing in Eureka Springs, Arkansas. The Biarritz was like my current car, but better, much better. The Biarritz was convertible and it had all the Cadillac touches: leather interior, power windows, command-control center dash, well positioned cup holders, etc.

This is not to say that I wouldn't miss my current car. After all, its working 8 track player has thrilled many a friend. Back in 1991, I wanted to buy a used car. I had my friends and family on the lookout. My girlfriend's mother called me from Sacramento to tell me about a car for sale:

HER: "I've found a great car for you. It's in great condition with low mileage, and it has had only one owner, an elderly woman who only drove it on Sundays. It's a bargain at only $1500."

ME: "Sounds great. What kind of car is it?"

HER: "A Ghia. A Ford Granada Ghia, 1978."

ME: "A Ghia? I'm not sure I know that car. What does it look like?" Totally clueless.

HER: "It's sporty. Two doors. Very attractive. It is a nice Burgundy color."

ME: "A Ghia, huh... Really. I think I can picture it," picturing a classic and sporty Karmann Ghia.

HER: "Yes Patrick, this car is a steal and it only has 42,000 miles on it. And, the owner just took it in and had $500 dollars' worth of touch up repairs on it. I saw the receipts. You should buy this car right away before someone else does. Do you want me to buy it and then you can ride up with Lisa this weekend and pick it up?" (I lived two hours away in San Francisco, and depended on my girlfriend Lisa for rides.)

ME: "Uhmmm.... Gosh that's very nice of you. Well.... You say it's a sporty classic, two-doors, and only 42,000 miles, eh? Uhmm.. yeah. Yes. Yes. For certain. Yes! I'd be crazy to say no. It sounds excellent. Thank you!! Buy it for me please."

And I hung up, the proud owner of a Burgundy Ghia!

Big, boat-sized cars are an acquired taste. I began learning that the minute I laid eyes on my Granada Ghia. It had two doors indeed, but each door was big and heavy enough to deflect cruise missiles. I wanted to cry when I first saw the car. I'd purchased a land-yacht, a battle ship, an aircraft carrier, and worst of all... an old ladies' car.

At first I tried to sell the car, and surprisingly it was very popular with the pimps and drug dealers who populated my neighborhood, but they never wanted to pony up enough money. Then, after a while, the unthinkable happened. I began to actually like the car. (A perverse case of 'If you can't beat em, join em'.)

Yes indeed, I began to brag about the police-cruiser like feel of its big 350 engine, the simulated leather, burgundy interior, and even the 14 miles to the gallon.

So Timothy and I are driving to Mexico in my Ghia, talking cars, and the 8-track is blaring (in mono) Kiss Alive II.

"Doctor! They call me Doctor Luv... (Doctor Luuuv!) I am your Doctor of Luv. I've got the cure!"

click-click

"Christine! Sixteen! She drives me crazy. I want to give her what I've got. There is no doubt about it. (I don't usually say things like this to a girl your age. But when I saw you coming out of school that day, I knew. I knew. I got to have ya. I got to have ya.) Christine!"

click-click

"Tomorrow and tonight! Tomorrow and tonight! We can rock all day. We can roll all night. Tomorrow and tonight! Tomorrow and tonight! Oh yeah. Uh-huh. All-riiiiiiiiiight!"

We pulled into our beach-resort destination and quickly found ourselves sitting in the sand talking with Andre, a German living in Baja. Andre was giving $25 trike rides to tourists—a trike being a motorized hang-glider able to take off and land on the beach.

Andre was like the turn-of-the-century man with a hot air balloon, who drops into the town square, waves his top-hat, and gives the first ride free to the Mayor. All marveled at his magnificent flying machine.

We'd been talking to Andre no longer than two minutes when out of the corner of my eye I see a long red convertible cruisin' down the beach. I swore that it was a Cadillac. Maybe even a Biarritz.

The car drove past and turned around. Tim and I jumped up to meet it. Sure enough it was a Cad. Riding low in the white interior saddle seats was a thin man wearing a tight, white muscle T-shirt and faded jeans. Sunglasses rested on top of his head. He was either a washed up Marlboro man, or a Vietnam Vet, and his shoulder was tattooed with an eagle.

ME: "What kind of Cad is this?" my eyes open wide with awe.

COWBOY: "She's a Biarritz. Like her?" He smiled and the sun glinted off his gold capped tooth.

ME: "Yeah! What year is it?"

COWBOY: "'83. And she's a chick magnet," one arm on the steering wheel. The other was stretched out over the head rest of the passenger seat, holding a can of beer.

I circled the car in astonishment while Tim talked dashboard features and quizzed the cowboy on his secret to not getting stuck in the sand.

COWBOY: "Oh yeah dude, a lot of people see me cruisin' out here and think they can do it with their Sport Utility Vehicles. They all get stuck and they can't figure how come I don't. Secret is to let most of the air out of your tires."

ME: "This is my dream car; right down to the year and color." I was practically drooling.

COWBOY: "Why don't you buy her from me dude? I'll sell her for $300." He took a hit off his Budweiser.

I had $320 in my wallet. It had never even crossed my mind that an entire working car could cost less than $1000. My mind was reeling. Tim fired back, "What about $200?"

COWBOY: "If you're serious and you've got $200 cash, I'd probably take you up on it. My name's Ron by the way. You'll see me out here cruisin' tomorrow and the next day, so come talk to me if you're serious." The red Cadillac pulled away, with surf crashing on the right and sand spinning lightly off the tires.

Instantly, Tim and I turned to one another and decided to buy the car, but by the time we finished talking about it, it was no longer in view.

We jumped into my Ghia and drove up the Mexican highway hoping that we'd be able to locate the Cadillac cowboy. I remembered seeing an old, run-down bar at the next exit and suggested that we try there first. Highway exits are quite different in Baja. They are only recognizable by a highly trained eye watching closely for a dirt road. No exit signs. No exit ramps. Just a dirt road you suddenly spot, and skid off onto. We found the cantina bar and our cowboy.

COWBOY: "So you came to buy my Cad?" and a grin flashed.

In the corner Mariachis were playing.

We pulled up a chair, bought Ron a beer and started with some questions.

TIM: "Where'd you get this car? Do you have the deed?"

COWBOY: "Yeah, I got the deed dudes. It IS my car, I didn't steal it. My friend didn't want it anymore because gas is really hard to get around here, so I bought it."

ME: "What's wrong with it?"

COWBOY: "Well, there's a lot of miles on the engine, she burns up a lot of oil, and the air conditioner don't work no more. But, for $200 what do you expect? And as you could see the interior alone is worth the price and more."

ME: "Will it make it back to San Diego?"

COWBOY: "Naw Duuude. You can't drive this car

to San Diego! It ain't legal. The Federales will stop you before you get to Rosarito."

TIM: "Why isn't it legal?"

COWBOY: "Cuz I chopped the top dude. I got shit faced drunk one night and took a saw to it. I broke two steel cutting blades tryin', so I got out my big ol' electric wood saw, with 1/4 teeth, and went at it. You shoulda seen it! Son-of-a-bitchin' sparks were flyin' all over the place and the roof came off. But it ain't legal dudes. Factory convertibles have roll bar reinforcement."

ME: "It looks right. Are you sure we couldn't get it back across the border?"

COWBOY: "Are you deaf dude? You can't take this car on the highway. The Federales have chased this car many times. They've never caught me, but they know this car. It's like Tom and Jerry around here. They chase you all day and then join you for a beer in the Cantina at night... Hey, I don't know how they can tell it ain't legal—I'd like to know what they teach cops at cop school—but cops can spot an illegal convertible from a mile away. The Cad is just for beach cruisin'."

I spoke quickly and quietly with Tim. $200 for a car that we couldn't drive on the highway suddenly didn't seem so hot.

ME: "What about a time-share arrangement?"

COWBOY: "A what dude?!"

TIM: "A time-share partnership agreement. Patrick and you co-own the car and he can use it whenever he comes to Mexico. You use it in the meantime."

COWBOY: "Yeah, well how much you going to pay me for that?"

ME: "Twenty-five bucks."

COWBOY: "You can't drive it on the highway and you gotta get some gas for it."

ME: "Deal."

Tim, well versed in contract language instructed me to flip over my paper placemat and start writing.

"PARTNERSHIP AGREEMENT

On 6/19/98 I hereby agree to enter into a partnership with Patrick Combs for the shared ownership and use of a 1983 Cadillac Biarritz (Modified) Burgundy in color. Terms of agreement are as follows, $25 for the rights to drive unencumbered through the beaches of Las Salinas, in perpetuity,..."

Right about here, Ron tensed up and asked, "Do I need to go get a lawyer for this?"

"...through the universe, until otherwise mutually agreed upon in writing, on a bar napkin here in La Salinas."

We both signed, shook hands and exchanged twenty-five dollars for the keys.

COWBOY: "You need to get some gas for the car. The closest gas station is 50 miles away."

ME: "How do people get gas around here?" surprised because we were in a town filled with at least a thousand cars.

COWBOY: "Bum some off friends. Buy some off tourists. Siphoning is a way of life down here."

ME: "I've got almost a full tank in my Ghia, out front. Can we siphon from it?"

COWBOY: "Yeah. Excellent. I'll get us a hose and can, but I can't suck the gas dudes. I got lung damage."

Before I could tell him he didn't have to suck the gas, he was lifting his T-shirt and pointing to a match box-shaped device implanted under the skin on his chest. I'd never seen anything like it before and I have no idea what it was. I don't want to know.

The three of us headed out of the cantina. As we exited the door, Ron asked another cowboy on the way in if he'd siphon some gas for us.

"No way," was the quick, swift answer.

I gathered by Ron's tone of voice that they were casual acquaintances. "Come on maaan—siphon for us. It won't take you long."

The man replied, "OK." I thought to myself, Did I miss the offer for a free beer, somewhere? What kind of persuasion technique was that??! 'These are not the droids you're looking for.' 'OK.'

Siphoning the gas from my car was easy, but oddly enough Ron decided to do it after all, for no apparent reason except enthusiasm. We funneled the gas into the Cad and after a few driving tips from Ron, Tim and I were cruisin the Baja Beach way.

It was a magnificent feeling. Seat back. Surf crashing just outside of the Cadillac door. Hands on the wheel. Feeling of ownership. Setting sun. Men, women, and children watching.

I couldn't resist the temptation instilled in me by who-knows-what movie. I traded seats with Tim and climbed out onto the hood for something I'd never done before: Hood surfing. Ta Da! This was my epiphany. With my knees bent and my arms outstretched, I was flying, and I felt good. Beach goers waved to me like I was in a parade. They probably figured I was waving back, but mostly I was trying to keep my balance.

The kookiest feeling in the world was parking the car on the beach in front of the resort, stepping out and walking past people relaxing by the pool.

How can I describe the surreal experience? Imagine taxiing an airplane to your local grocery store. Getting out of the plane, cruising inside to get some chips, and

107

then taxiing back to your home. It just isn't supposed to happen, but it's very fun.

It was a stop for some refreshments. With drinks in hand, we got back into our Cad and resumed cruising. Tim took his turn at Hood Surfin' and one upped me by doing it with a drink in his hand. No spillage, even through the occasional swerve for children at play.

We drove that Cad up and down the beach until the sun went down. Then we figured we oughta return it to Ron for the night. But Ron was nowhere to be found at the Cantina. So we resumed cruisin'.

In the darkness, on the drive back to our Palapa (large umbrellas provided by the resort to put your tent under), Tim discovered a speedway: A whole new driving lane, now available because of low tide. The wet packed sand meant we could go much faster. Much faster. 65 miles per hour through the darkness. Vaarrr-rooooooooooooooom!

A mile and a half of beach in a very little time. Then we turn around and Vaarrrrooooooooooooom! All the way back to the other end. Scarier and more exciting than any ride I've been on at Disney or Universal.

We were on our third pass when, for an instant our headlights illuminated a waving, screaming man in white. We sped by him catching only a glimpse and a bite of sound, "You @!*#! Sto..."

I yelled over the roaring engine, "That might be my partner Ron, but I couldn't tell at that speed. It also might be someone else who wants to beat the shit out of us, so go back, but don't slow down too much. I'll try and get a better look."

Again our headlights lit up the waving, screaming man, and it was our gringo Cowboy. Still he had a beer in his hand.

He was yelling all kinds of things at a very rapid rate. "You @!*#! give me my car! What the hell are you doing driving it so fast?! You @!*#! , where the hell were you?!! Give me my @!*#! car! I gave you guys a good deal and you're @!*#! with me."

TIM: "Chill out homey. We're not hurting the car. It's OK, we're driving where the sand is packed down. It's cool. The car's fine. And you got $25 and a beer for loaning out your car."

ME: "Hey, we didn't mean to upset you or hurt your car. Tim give him the keys to his car. Ron, you're the last guy we want to upset. You're our friend. Take your car. Sorry."

Our duel answers didn't calm Ron down. He kept yelling frantically. "This @!*#! car is a cruiser. Give me my @!*#! car. You @!*#! disappeared with my car and now you're ruining it. It's just for cruising. Low speeds man. None of this shit."

Tim and I both basically repeated ourselves, and Ron revealed which tact he preferred.

"@!*#! you," he said pointing at Tim. "I know your type. You twist everything to make it seem the other way around. You're just like my brother. @!*#! you."

Then he turned to me and said, "I just didn't know where you guys were. And when I told my mom about our deal she started calling me @!*#! stupid. She kept telling me I was stupid to trust you guys, and that I'd never see my car again. Then I went to my girlfriend's and she told me I was stupid too. And since I couldn't find you guys anywhere, what was I supposed to think? Everyone's calling me stupid and I thought, probably I am. You understand?"

ME: "Yeah, I totally understand. Everyone's telling you that you were stupid for trusting us and you didn't

know if we'd stolen your car. But look who was right Ron,
you were. You could trust us. We weren't going to steal
your car. We looked for you at the cantina but couldn't
find you. Anyway dude, take your car. We're sorry."

Ron didn't take the keys. Instead he took a hit off
his beer and said, "What time are you guys gonna cruise
tomorrow? There's going to be a party of 1000 people
here and I wanna cruise with you."

Eventually Ron disappeared down the beach, and
left the Cad with us for the next three days. Tim and I
laughed ourselves to sleep under the Palapa. 'Only in
Mexico!' is what I believe we kept repeating.

Today my son and I were hiding behind the car together during a Nerf gun battle. He's four. He suggested a plan. We high-fived to confirm it. Then he says...

"Dad, keep the plan in your mind! ... Don't let it slip out of your ears."

Live, Really Live

(From my journal after a triumphant run of my budding comedy show, 'Man 1, Bank 0'.)

Well, I dreamed, I dared, I did. And what a feeling I have now throughout my body.

To fulfill a dream that originated from your heart is deeply satisfying. To see yourself rise to a new level of your very best is a truly peaceful and awesome feeling. To live something out that you know took all your courage and all your inner-resources—is, as the U2 song sings, 'the sweetest thing'.

I enjoyed almost every show I did here, but last night's show—my final night's show—was an immensely triumphant personal experience. I performed better than I've ever performed.

In each of the six shows prior to my last, I kept trying to hit a sharpness and timing that I knew I could do in my heart, but that kept eluding me over and over. (Our triumphs require we work hard for them.) But last night—last night I hit it!

It felt like finding a new fire that I possessed on the inside.

I so deeply encourage you to pursue the most exciting and scary dreams you have in your heart. The rewards are so immense and have nothing to do with money.

It's funny - the dream in my mind's eye about this one-man show was entirely about achieving a high level of performance. When I'd see a person's performance that wowed me, on the inside I'd hear a voice that said, "You could do that." It both excited me and scared the shit out me—for years.

I also tacked on the dream of performing in New York City and seeing my show on HBO, but those were just mental tack-ons—goals to shoot for that I figured would reflect that I'd really arrived as a performer.

In my heart, and in my gut, I knew my dream was about holding an audience spellbound and laughing for more than an hour with a story. If I could do that, it would be all the reward.

I've lived that dream now and I realize I was wrong. The reward for braving your dream and seeing it through is so much bigger and richer and brighter and better.

Don't get me wrong; to have seen my performance dream come true is a feeling I'll take to my grave; so deeply affirming, joyous and great for my self-confidence. But what we tend to overlook when deciding whether to go for our dream or not, are all the side benefits—braving your dream will introduce you to new friends, take you to wonderful places, open entire new worlds, treat you to incredible surprises, and enrich you as a person.

But most of all—and the greatest side benefit of all for seeing your dream through—is the feeling I had all week on the inside: a great lovingness. A great big lovingness for life, for myself, for people, for places, for simply being...

It is so self-loving to live out the Highest Grandest Visions you have in the heart of your soul, that the PRI-

MARY reward will always be a Grand Loving Feeling on the inside for all. Lovingness for yourself, for others, and for all that surrounds you.

Imagine your life when you feel so good on the inside that lovingness is your primary feeling; imagine all the magic created by that lovingness! Feelings of Lovingness can only create and attract supreme goodness. The more lovingness you feel, the more riches you attract—and give!

Here I am at the peak of a mountain—having scaled to a new height of my dreams—but surprisingly, the best reward isn't the altitude, or even the view—it's the lovingness I feel inside, and what a feeling! It's a double-reward: your dreams come true and this spiritual-satisfaction!

I'll try to exceed my best again next performance, and so the goals will be reset, but this lovingness is permanent. It is broadcast into the world and guaranteed by Universal Law to ripple on forever doing good for all. That's what I call True Success.

Love yourself so much that you believe in your dreams. Your Highest Grandest Ambitions are the Truth. They are the truth about who you are and what you can do. And they are waiting—waiting on the edge of their seats—to love you back with support, magical assistance, new-found courage, synchronicity, serendipity, opportunity, new worlds, new friends, and dreams come true.

Be good to yourself—really good.

Notice all the beauty around you—in people, in places, from the plants to the stars.

And live - really live,

Love, Patrick

There Will Be Miracles

She was looking for something. She'd been looking for 9 months.

I had just arrived at the San Francisco Fringe Festival after a year of failure. I'd been trying to develop my first comedy show, titled "Man 1, Bank 0." I'd failed with the story in about 10 classrooms coast to coast. One of those was at a community college in Chicago where a teacher let me take over.

After a dismal performance in the corner of the classroom, I heard one student say to the other on their way out the door, "I'd rather have taken a test than sit through that shit." It was a low point among many humiliating failures that year while trying to develop my show.

Being at the SF Fringe Festival was both a blessing and curse for me. A blessing because it was my first time to perform in an actual theatre. The SF Fringe was a lottery, no talent required, perfect for me. I got in based on luck of the draw. It was also a curse because now I would be bombing in front of paying audiences in a real theatre. The stakes were higher. The fall was longer.

She was in San Francisco to try and find what she was looking for, but she did not find it and her next stop was a flight out of Oakland, California.

My first show at the Fringe Festival was for a late night audience of 7, three of which were critics from San Francisco newspapers. I sucked and they responded to my performance accordingly.

My second show the following day was even later at night for only 5 people. I was not good but I did relax into the performance a little more than I ever had. I was getting over any bad feelings I had about how bad I was.

I enjoyed trying to do the show and being in a real theatre for the first time so much that even doing it poorly was satisfying in a strange way.

Right before my third show, I peeked out from behind the curtain and saw a good twenty people in my audience, which gave me a half-full theatre! It also scared me to death.

I wanted to be good at entertaining a theatre audience with a story more than I had wanted anything else in my life, but all I had done was suck for a year. The last thing I wanted to do was repeat the same mistakes in front of my largest comedy audience yet. I had a hard talk with myself that was long overdue behind the curtain.

"Patrick, what are you doing here..?"

I'm just trying to tell a funny story...

"Then stop making it so complicated. You can tell stories, so get out there and tell the story—Be yourself!"

I had been putting too much pressure on myself to be funny all year. I did need to just relax and be myself. I went out and did my third show better than I'd ever done before—people were cracking up and I finally got real applause at the end of my show.

For me it was absolutely exhilarating! I was on cloud nine after that show.

The woman looking for someone got delayed in the city and had to reschedule her flight. Now she had time to kill in San Francisco.

Doing well on my third show filled me with a bliss I'd never known. Clearly, I'd only made a small audience at a small festival laugh, but it didn't curb my enthusiasm a bit. I felt on the inside like I'd crushed it at Carnegie Hall! And I was so happy that I was overflowing with love and joy.

As I stood around other performers the next day, I noticed that on the inside I was wishing that each one of them would also have the greatest success of their life. It was like I had more happiness than one person could contain and it had to be shared with others.

My fourth show sold out and I was funnier than I'd ever been. Then like a miracle, the audience gave me a standing ovation. If someone had interrupted and told me this was heaven, I would have believed them.

My fifth show also sold out and it garnered me my second standing ovation. If there were a measuring instrument for joy, I would have maxed it out. I'd never been as happy in my life.

The woman needing to kill time noticed posters for the SF Fringe Festival. She thought seeing a show might be a good way to kill time until her flight. She went to the ticket counter and got a ticket for a show starting in about an hour that was selling out every night.

My sixth and final show not only sold out, but many people who hoped to get a ticket were turned away. Before my show started, the festival director came into my dressing room and said that "Man 1, Bank 0" had won the Festival Sell-Out award and Festival Favorite award.

I sat there completely stupified. My show was an abject failure for a year before coming to this festival. I almost quit right before applying to get into the SF Fringe. Now I was walking out for another sold out show. The show went magnificently and I received my third standing ovation.

Standing there receiving my applause, I had no idea how I'd ever get another show, but I could have died happy if this was the last one I ever got to do. I felt like I'd summited my Everest.

At a Fringe Festival you go from star to janitor the second your show is over because you have only 5 minutes to clear the stage for the next act. As my final audience was filing out of the small black box theatre, I was on my hands and knees in front of them picking up pieces of paper I had strewn across the stage during my show, calendar pages that marked time during the story.

So there I was picking up trash when a woman tapped me on the shoulders and said, "You were funny. We should talk." My response to her displayed the insecurity I still had. "It's a funny story, thank you."

The woman who had been looking for something spoke to me again, "No You were funny. Here's my card, call me." I was in such a rush to clear my stage that I pushed her business card into my pocket without even so much as glancing at it.

I walked back to my hotel alone right after my show. I swear to God my feet might not have been touching the ground I felt so joyful, happy and fulfilled. My heart was overflowing with a pure love for life; a love that feels like the deepest peace and the highest high.

"Follow your Bliss!", Joseph Campbell said. I'd followed mine into comedy and I had caught up to it. It was every bit as wonderful and worth it as I'd ever imagined.

As I glided home through the streets of San Francisco, I remembered the woman and her business card. I took it from my pocket and saw the letters, HBO.

The woman had been looking for something for nine months, all over the country. She was a talent scout for HBO *and the U.S. Comedy Arts Festival held annually in Aspen, Colorado. She was looking for the funniest new comedy acts in America.*

Soon after, I was performing in Aspen with Jack Black, Joe Rogan, Diane Keaton, Sarah Jessica Parker, Louis C.K. and many, many more comedy legends. I couldn't believe I was there.

HBO had never sent a talent scout to the San Francisco Fringe Festival before. *Ever.* And the woman had not intended to see any shows at it. You could say she was at my show quite by coincidence or luck. But I think she got there by another means:

"Where there is great love, there are always miracles." —Willa Cather

Infinity and Beyond

I had no intention of getting a new car when my 6 year old son, Will, and I took my 8 year old Infiniti into the dealership for a minor repair. But between seeing the new 2015 model—all shiny black and muscled up—and discovering it was an eco-friendlier car because of a hybrid engine, I spontaneously traded in my white Infiniti and drove off the lot that same day with a slick new black one.

Will and I quickly nicknamed the new car the Batmobile. Not only because it looked fitting for Batman on the outside, but because it had an extraordinary dashboard console of high tech screens and incredible electronics. To say we were both dazzled by the sophisticated array in front of us would be an understatement! We loved the turbo power boost and we were sure one of the buttons must be an eject function.

You could call me a raving fan of Infiniti and you'd be right. My first new car ever was the Infiniti I'd spontaneously traded in. Infiniti and I were love at first sight.

Although it's silly to love a car, I loved it and enjoyed driving it for 8 years. And I was always deeply impressed by Infiniti's customer service. Quality car. Quality service.

Now, my wife had kindly obliged me the spontaneous trade in of our family car. It was shockingly uncharacteristic of me to lease a new car without my wife seeing it, let alone us both taking at least half a year to fully consider a new car purchase—We're conservative that way.

So imagine her shock when I phoned her from the dealership and said, "Honey, I really, really want to trade in our old Infiniti for this new black one that Will and I are looking at—and I really want to do it today so we have it for our trip to Arizona tomorrow.

"Can you please be okay with that? I promise you, you're going to love the car. It's amazing *and it's a hybrid* so it's kinder to Earth."

She was indeed shocked I was asking her to agree to such a thing. But I was even more shocked when she said, "Okay. Since you really want it, you should just do it."

I won't tell you she said this with any enthusiasm, but she did say it. And that's how it came to be that Will and I pulled into our driveway *in The Batmobile.*

The next morning our family of four headed out to the driveway for a trip to our daughter Alyssa's dance competition in Phoenix. It was road trip time in the new car. I was so excited about The Batmobile wowing the girls just as it had wowed Will and me the night before.

Deanna didn't say a word about the slick exterior and Alyssa said "I don't like the black color." Strike one!

When everyone climbed in, my wife was unusually quiet until she said, "I don't prefer black interiors because they show dirt so easily and get hot." Strike Two!

Okay, two strikes against the car, I thought, but I hadn't started it up. They hadn't heard the growl of the powerful engine. And if that wasn't enough, I was positive they'd both be completely won over by the car when we hit the freeway and they experienced the self-driving mode. That's right, self-driving biatch!

Infiniti's have a push button starter. Press the button and the car comes to life. I aimed my finger at the glowing white button and declared, "Okay family, meet The Batmobile!" And with that I pressed the button.

Nothing.

The Batmobile was dead in the driveway.

"You'd think a new car would at least start," Deanna said. "I'm not impressed."

Her words were searing. To say it was embarrassing would be an understatement.

"I'll call Infiniti," I said and everyone piled out of the car. We sat on steps up to our porch, waiting for Infiniti to bring a loaner. They came within an hour, brought us an SUV loaner and towed The Batmobile away.

Climbing into the loaner was a real low point for me. But apparently not for the girls. They commented on the fact that it was much roomier than The Batmobile, that they loved the interior, that it was a great family car... Just shoot me.

Infiniti called me a few days later. I was informed that they found nothing wrong with the car, and guessed it was probably just a dead battery. They replaced the battery for free—just in case it had been sitting on the lot too long before I bought it.

I got the car back and there was very little fanfare from the girls about the car's return in working order.

You really do only get one chance to make a first impression. And The Batmobile had epically failed.

As a matter of fact, my wife had not yet driven in the Infiniti when, two days later, I exited a coffee shop after spending a couple hours chatting with a friend, only to find the Infiniti dead again!

It gave me a sick feeling in my stomach, that something was wrong with my new car. I hated the thought of telling my wife. But Infiniti responded quickly with a loaner and a tow.

Deanna was kind. "Something's wrong with that car and obviously they better fix it this time."

Infiniti called me a couple days later. "Mr. Combs, your car is ready for pick up. This time we ran a full diagnostics check on it. And we don't want you to feel bad, it could happen to anyone, but the problem is you're not turning off the car..."

I'm not turning off the car..?

I was stunned to hear the words. How could I not be turning off the car?

"How do you know I'm not turning off the car?" I asked.

"The car has a computer that records all the car's activities and the computer tells us it's being left on. It's understandable. You're probably just distracted by all the cool electronics."

My relationship with The Batmobile started to flash before my eyes. The first night when Will and I brought it home after dark, I sat in the car marveling at the dazzling futuristic dashboard which looked its absolute best in the black of night. God, did I just exit the car without turning it off?

The day I stepped into the coffee shop and sat for an extra few minutes pushing buttons to learn their cool functions, to marvel at the car's ability to record the minute by minute use of the hybrid motor.

Did I really forget to turn off the car?

It seemed improbable because turning off a car is such an automatic action. But on the other hand, I am a very spacey person. Only my family knows this about me, but maybe the Batmobile's onboard computer was now turning my hidden flaw into hard published data.

"Okay, I'll be in to pick up the car," I replied. "And Good Lord, I'll be sure and turn it off from now on. I'm so sorry. I do love the electronics in this car. Apparently too much."

Surprisingly, I wasn't embarrassed. The thought of my spacey-ness being the problem just made me laugh at myself. And at the same time, it was hard for me to accept what the computer had determined. Who's to say a computer's right?

My wife on the other hand, she *Loved* the news! She was like, "That's sooooo YOU! Only *You* would walk away with the car still on!" Quickly, she was on the phone spreading the story to her friends. "The problem was... He's not turning off the car! This is what I've had to live with for 20 years!"

"I don't know if that's true Deanna. It's just what the computer said. I think I'm turning off the car," I said in defense of myself.

Deanna wasn't buying it so I turned to my son. "Will, I'm turning off the car. You can't always believe computers."

"I believe you Dad," he said with the naive sincerity of a child.

When I picked up the car from the dealership, I brought donuts and apologized for the trouble. They were really nice and said no problem.

The car started fine after that. I was conscious about turning it off. Will would even help remind me. It was all good. We finally had a reliable Batmobile, because seemingly I was finally not distracted so intensely by the electronics.

And then, two weeks later, I came out again to a dead car that wouldn't start. And if I'm being honest, I couldn't tell you if I had or had not remembered to turn off the car before it died. I'd guess that I had, but I couldn't be sure. So that was an embarrassing call to make to Infiniti!

Infiniti kindly again towed the car and gave me a loaner at no cost. Then days later, they yet again informed me that the problem was *driver error*. The computer proved it. And then Infiniti's service manager on the phone said the unexpected, "Mr. Combs, did we teach you to turn off the car when you bought it?"

"Uhm, no you didn't. But it seems pretty simple. If I'm correct, you just press the on/off button. The exact same way I turned off my previous Infiniti successfully—for 8 years," I replied.

"Well Mr. Combs, when you come in to pick up your car we'll train you on it just in case," the voice on the other end of the phone said back.

I found his proposition absolutely delightful! The thought of someone at Infiniti teaching me to press a button was not something I was going to miss!

The next day I was at the dealer and sitting in The Batmobile with a man from sales in the driver's seat. "Mr. Combs, this is how you turn off the car—press this button!"

I could barely keep a straight face. "Can you just do that again, so I can be sure I got it." And he did. And then I tried it. And we had a laugh together in the car.

My wife continued to think my not turning off the car was the funniest thing EVER. She continued to tell the story to family friends and although I recognized what a funny story it was, I remained unsure I was the problem. The computer's opinion was more suspect to me than ever before. I'm spacey, but not *that* spacey, I thought to myself.

The Batmobile died two more times in the next month. This pushed me to develop a redundant system for making certain I turned off the car every time I got out of it.

"Will, I'm pressing the off button."

"Check!" my son would reply, visually witnessing my action. "Dad, are you sure you hit the button?"

"Yes son, I'm sure I hit the button."

And then one day it happened. After Will and I did our car-off, double-check, once out of the car, I looked through the window and saw the car dashboard still on! This time, Will and I both were 100% positive I'd turned it off!

We'd caught the car malfunctioning.

"Will, you saw I turned off the car, right?!"

"Right Dad!"

"That proves it's car error son! Car error not Dad error!"

"Right Dad! Car error!"

Within seconds I was on the phone with Infiniti's headquarters in Franklin, Tennessee. Their customer service agent was happily listening to the details of my story until I called the car a lemon.

Apparently, saying lemon to Infiniti is like pulling a fire alarm.

"Mr. Combs, I'll have an Infiniti lawyer get in touch with you." And within a day, a lawyer called me and said he'd been assigned to my case! He informed me that Infiniti would be sending an Investigative Engineer out to my local dealership to inspect the problem with my car.

I got off the phone relieved that I would soon convince both my dealer and my wife that the car was the problem, not me. I wanted to return the car under California's Lemon laws.

Two weeks later, Infiniti's lawyer phoned me. "Mr. Combs, our Investigative Engineer flew out to San Diego and did a thorough investigation of your car. He concluded the same thing as the dealer, you're not turning it off. The computer data is clear and exact. Our case is closed on this, but we are going to put another new battery in it."

I was incredulous. "Listen, I'm 100% positive your computer is wrong. Start your investigation over, and call me when you've figured out that the car is a lemon and you're ready to buy it back. I need to set the record straight with my wife! I'm losing all credibility."

My stern words worked. He reluctantly agreed to send another investigative engineer from Franklin. A couple weeks later, the lawyer left a message on my voice mail. The second engineer came back with the same conclusion. Driver error. Investigation closed.

My local dealer wanted their loaner back. I hated to give it because I knew it would conclude my case and leave me forever with the faulty new car. Never again would Infiniti give me a loaner or try and fix the Batmobile. But all hope was lost so I scooped up Will and returned to my local Infiniti dealer on a Friday afternoon.

I walked up to Adam in Service. He knew me all too well, presumably as his idiot customer, but he was always kind.

I handed him the keys to the loaner.

"Sorry Patrick. Even I wanted to believe you. But the good news is we've been starting your car fine every day for two weeks now. It's all good to go. I'll retrieve it for you." And he went to get my car.

Will and I sat in the lobby waiting. "It's okay Dad. I believed you there for a while, but now I'll help you remember to turn off the car. You're still a good Dad and a great person." His exact words.

When times are tough, you learn who your true friends are.

Apparently the service department was very busy because Will and I waited quite a while for Adam to return with The Batmobile.

He finally walked up to me, looked down at the floor, and sheepishly said, "Uhm, we're going to put you back in the loaner, because your car won't start."

Will burst into a laugh before I could!

"Did I train you on how to turn it off, Adam?" I said with a joking smile.

Adam chuckled, shook his head, and said he had already reported the error to Infiniti Headquarters in Franklin. I called and told my wife the redeeming news immediately. It was a personal victory for me.

The next day, Infiniti's lawyer phoned and informed me that he had begun the paper work to buy back my car. And a week later they did.

I needed a new car and figured the manager of my local Infiniti dealer was going to make me a really sweet offer for all my trouble. But that never came. As a matter of fact, the manager never even bothered to see me or say anything to me at all.

Infinity offered me a courtesy ride to wherever I wanted. I had them take me to BMW.

I got BMW's all-electric car, the i3. The kids and I nicknamed it "Tron."

I absolutely love driving an electric car. So far the computer hasn't accused me of any errors.

Our friend bought a new Infiniti a week after we returned ours. Will put his hand on it and said, "Sorry to tell you this, but you bought a lemon!"

Sorry Infiniti. I think he's tainted for life.

A Very Pink Room

There is *A Lot* of *Pink* in this room! I actually don't even know where I am tonight but somewhere in a Bed & Breakfast outside a little village town called Millom where I performed at a place called The Beggars Theatre this evening. And my room is pink, pink, pink. We drew straws and I got the pink ladies room. So by morning I should be fully in my feminine.

The road into this area was gorgeous beyond belief with all the green rolling hills and sheep and old stone walls; but also thin, curvy, narrow, winding, and incredibly deadly—as made apparent by two road signs that said exactly:

"1,542 deaths in 5 years on this road. Drive carefully"

That's almost one death a day! On a short section of road that seems remote enough to only entertain a few cars a day. I don't like those odds.

Then we pass the next sign forty sheep down that says, and I quote:

"Oncoming vehicles in the middle of the road".

Well that explains the high death rate! Cars coming

down the middle of a thin road towards you do tend to kill. Why not a sign that says, *"Stop driving down the middle of the road!"*

But we made it. We pull in and there's a statue of a coal miner shoveling coal into a mining cart right in front of the theater. A plaque underneath said,

"Poet" and a name. So later I say to the theater director, a really lively high spirited woman, "So that coal miner was a poet?"

She says, "No, just a coal miner."

So I ask, "Why does it say under him, "Poet"?

And she says, "Does it really?? I have no idea because that guy was just a coal miner."

So apparently the town saved money by adding a plaque about a poet to a statue about a miner, two birds with one stone sort of thing... Too bad because I had an entire romantic narrative worked out in my head about a Poet Coal Miner.

Anyway, great audience and great show here tonight, ton of laughing—and then after the show it got even better. The theater director took us to the local pub a few miles out of town on a dark country road. And upon walking into it, my first thought was, 'My God look where I am, somewhere in the UK, in a tiny village, in a local pub with the locals, all six of them...'

This is part of what makes touring so amazingly special.

Then the pint drinking began and it was just one of those laughing nights. We all about fell off our stools laughing so hard for hours. I remember only a few of the things we laughed about. One, when it came out that the theater director had been promoting me around town (and to the bartender Dave) as the "American Con-Artist who put one over on the bank."

At first I thought he said American Comic. But nope, here I was promoted as a Con-Artist, which was apparently the right angle because the theatre was packed. So in a village called Millom in Britain, I am known as a con-man which apparently is a really good thing.

Anyway, the whole tour is delightful from the driving views, to the great audiences, to the great laughing sessions we have every night in pubs. And today we managed to avoid "oncoming vehicles in the middle of the road" to live another day. But wow is this room pink.

Good night pink room. Good night pink lamp. Good night pink blanket. Good night pink curtains. Good night pink tissues. Good night pink sheets. Good night pink tea set. Good night pink "for ladies'" basket in the pink bathroom. By morning I'll probably be menstruating.

AMF

"AMF" was written in felt pen on the back of my Adidas running shoes. I told my mother it stood for "Adios, My Friend" But that wasn't true at all—It stood for something much more vulgar. Actually, all the guys on my high school cross country team had it emblazoned on their shoes that year—it did the trick, of making us feel cool.

It was my senior year and I was headed for the Oregon State Cross Country Championship Meet for the first time in my four-year running career. All I had to do was place in the top 8 at the Central Oregon District Meet—an easy task, considering I was a shoe-in for second place.

The only guy in the entire district of twelve schools that was better than me was Eric Martin. Eric Martin: Perfectly lean, 6-foot 2-inch runner's body that was also superb in track, basketball, and downhill skiing.

I don't remember what triggered the thought that I could beat Eric Martin despite the fact that he'd beaten me in each of our six previous races against one another. But something deep inside of me concluded that I could win the District Meet with a mind-over-matter strategy.

And then, during the week preceding the District Meet, I went somewhat insane—I became obsessed, possessed and entirely focused on a single mental rehearsal: me outracing Eric Martin.

Mentally convincing myself that I could run faster than Eric Martin was actually hard for the first few days. I'd close my eyes and try to imagine myself running in front of Eric, but instead my mind would place Eric in front of me. But persistence endured, and I eventually had a mental break-through. For three days prior to the District Meet, I'd close my eyes and Eric Martin would be chasing me, forced to read the three letters, AMF, on the back of my shoe.

The District Meet was held in Ontario, Oregon, four hours away from my high school in Bend. It was on a Saturday in October, and an immaculate Saturday at that, all blue sky and sunshine.

The race began at 1 P.M. and I felt tremendous from head to toe. At the starting line, I was lined up amongst 23 other guys. It was a proud feeling, being able to look up and down that line, at tall runners, short runners, thin runners, thick runners, and know that, despite how "perfect for running" so many of them looked, I could and would finish ahead of them all.

With the exception of Eric Martin, I'd already beaten each of them repeatedly. I saved sizing Eric Martin up for last—because I knew it would be a test of mental preparedness. He was on my right in his school colors of red and black, and when I looked at his 6-foot 2-inch frame, 3 inches taller than my own, my mind again pictured him trailing far behind me. AMF.

The course was 3.1 miles through a state park, with green grass, dirt trails, and rolling hills—it would take the winner about 15 minutes and forty-five seconds to run. *It would take Eric a bit longer.*

It is nerve-wracking, nerve-wracking, nerve-wrack-

ing at the starting line. And then the gun goes off—
BANG!

Everything starts silently moving, and you hear
nothing for the first minute or so. Then, with a little
more breathing room, your mind starts to hear your
feet hitting, your breath exhaling, and your competitors
crowding. A few minutes later, your focus shifts inward
to your thoughts, your strategies, your pain.

A lot of runners kept pace with Eric and myself for
the first mile. Only a few were still somewhat near us at
the two-mile mark, and they faded out fast.

It was only Eric and me with just under a mile to
go, and I was breathing down his neck. Being behind
him was a smart move; I was "drafting" him, a strategy
where you make your competitor fight the wind while
you conserve energy.

Everything was working the way I'd imagined it—
right down to being able to instantly dispel the lazy
little suggestions that every runner's mind whispers
up during an exhaustive race; thoughts like "drop out
and pretend like you rolled your ankle" or "slow down a
bit—who's going to know the difference." My mind was
too busy singing a favorite song by the pop-rock band,
Cheap Trick:

"No one's going to give it away. They make it hard
for the people today. To get what you want, you've got
to do it yourself. Don't be afraid to drive the nail in the
wood; Or drink the water that ta-tastes so good. You'll
go the distance, you never thought that you could. Reach
out and take it. Reach out and ta-ta-ta-take it. Reach out
and take it, oh yeah!"

We turned a corner, and Eric increased his speed.
So did I.

We went another eighth of a mile or so and Eric increased his speed again.

Despite the fact that I already was running a faster pace than any race before, and feeling it in my side, I increased my speed as well.

Every race has a do-or-die point. With half a mile to go, and only a few steps behind Eric, I thought to myself, "It's now or never; time to wish Señor Martin a Spanish farewell. Adios!"

I kicked up my speed and passed him. If he was looking down, Eric could now see "AMF" written on the back of my shoes.

Apparently it motivated him because suddenly he sped up and burst past me. I pushed myself to go as fast as I could possibly go, screaming on the inside from pain, but I could not keep up.

As a matter of fact, I couldn't even stay standing up. Coming down a slight hill one hundred yards from the finish line, for the first time in all of my races, my legs gave out from underneath me and I collapsed to the grass.

At first I was in shock, I couldn't believe I was lying on the ground. From the turf, I saw Eric break the finish-line tape. I got back up and began to lurch forward. Where once I had two strong legs, I now had two rickety stilts. Like a drunk, I managed to stumble another twenty yards or so and then I fell down again.

I began to feel embarrassed; conscious of the fact that busloads of coaches, guys, and girls were watching me do the drop. I tried to stand back up, only this time I absolutely could not. My legs simply had no more bone in them—nothing but noodles.

It took only one sight to snap me out of my own self-consciousness: a runner dashed passed me. Suddenly I thought, "Third place". It was an outcome I'd never considered. I began to crawl.

I was crawling as fast as I could when another runner passed me. "Fourth place," I thought. I kept crawling and two runners, racing neck and neck, passed me. "Sixth place... Only the top eight finishers go to State."

Panic! Panic! Panic! I was crawling as fast as I could, when another runner sped past me. "Seventh place."

With a shot of strength that I don't know where I got, I managed to get back onto my feet. I wasn't exactly running again; I felt as if my entire body was encased in cement, but I was at a slow walker's pace. I'll never forget Neil Anderson, dressed in a purple and yellow track outfit, a guy I'd beaten before while I was sick, passing me up, and forever eliminating me from running in the Oregon State Cross Country Championships.

For the record, I stumbled across the line in twelfth place. Add to the record the fact that, for the next two hours, I lay packed in ice and wrapped in a blue tarp, convulsing, dry heaving, and wishing for a quick painless death to alleviate the aching, squeezed, and wrung-out feeling I had from head to toe.

When I could finally be moved, we boarded the bus, back for home. I cried the entire evening ride. My coach said it was one of the greatest efforts he'd ever seen from an athlete, and he said that I suffered from heat stroke, which is caused from not drinking enough water. At first I replied, "No way, because I did drink a lot of fluids the day of the race." But then he explained that race day is too late; the body needs a lot of fluids the entire week prior to a race—a good measure I had failed to do.

By Monday, I was back at school and feeling better. I was disappointed not to be going to State, but I'd found strength in the realization that I'd pushed myself to my very limits. The District Meet was my first experience in truly giving something everything I had.

That same day I was sitting in my seventh-period science class, the last class of the day, when I was called to the front office. When I got there, I was greeted by a sports reporter from the city newspaper and interviewed for a feature story about my District Meet run. The next day, for the first time in my life, my story was being told in the city newspaper, and it was full of positive remarks and sincere praise about my run.

Of course years have passed since I tried to beat Eric Martin, and that race has taken on special significance to me. From it, I learned that you can live with a loss when you gave it your all; it's the giving it your all that protects you from regret.

Before that race, I, and everyone else, knew that I could go to State. But what I didn't know about myself was if I could push myself to my very limits. After the race, I had zero doubt that I gave that race my absolute all. Doing your best is the only option—even if it results in failure.

And Eric, if you're reading this, there's something I've wanted to tell you for a long time (after the race I was too busy barfing up a lung): "For you, AMF on the back of my shoes stands for Awesome My Friend!"

Red Dress, Blue Dress

"Which dress do you want to wear Alyssa?" Standing in the front room, I could hear my wife struggling in our daughter's bedroom to get Alyssa to choose a dress to wear. Alyssa was two at the time. "I don't know mommy. I don't know," I could hear her say in her perfectly sweet little voice. Finally my wife gave up. "Go ask your father which one he likes."

Down the hall my sweet daughter came toddling, looking adorable as ever and holding a blue dress in one hand and a red dress in the other. She stopped in front of me, her hair in a ponytail.

"Daddy, which one do you like?" she asked.

Of course I hardly preferred one dress over the other. I just loved the little girl in the middle. But I chose, "I like the blue one honey." I thought she might agree or disagree but instead she turned around without a word and began returning to her room.

"Which one are you going to wear Alyssa?" her mother called out again.

Without skipping a beat, Alyssa replied, "I'm going to wear the red one."

There it was. The opposite of my opinion.

And then she said, "Daddy's going to wear the blue one."

You're Saving Our Kids

(I wrote this for Deanna, the mother of my children, but it's clearly for all good mothers...)

It's mother's day and my wife, the mother of our two children, deserves all the credit, compliments, and love in the world on this day. Deanna is truly an extraordinary mother, by all accounts. She is tender, she is loving, she is attentive, she is kind, she is intelligent in her approach, and she is tireless. But on this day, I'm thinking less about what she gives our children, and more about what she's saving them from...

Thank God for Deanna because without her:

Our kids would go to school dirty, since I only think to bathe them once a week—and only if I think the dirt is thick enough to impair their vision or warrant a fine.

Thank God for Deanna because without her:

Our kids would both have been raised in bags, not clothes. Because I think a bag would make it easier to change a diaper. I think pants over diapers is ridiculous.

PS—Turns out they sell bags like this for kids—someone gifted us one, but my wife insists it's only for sleeping in (or maybe she said sledding) and she refused to put our baby in it - so our baby actually has style and will learn to walk because of his mother.

Thank God for Deanna because without her:

Alyssa would never have learned to tell time.

Rather than explain the clock, I thought it was easier to just tell her that time was actually an artificial construct, that it wasn't real. I was so proud when she told her teacher, "My dad says 'Only the now is real.'" Deanna was not impressed.

Thank God for Deanna because without her:

Our kids would have no friends.

All our friends with kids come through Deanna.

Actually, when I think about it, ALL our friends come from Deanna. Our kids wouldn't know there was such thing as "friends" if not for their mom.

Thank God for Deanna because without her:

Our kids wouldn't know how to swim. Or dance. Or ski. Or anything, for that matter, that I anticipated in advance that I one day might not be in the mood to do with them.

Like swimming the other day. I didn't want to go in with Alyssa. The water was too cold. But I had to. It was awful. So I vowed to not teach Will to swim. I'd just tell him later that he didn't want to learn to swim when he was little, no matter how hard I tried.

But you watch his mother is going to teach him. And I'll have to get in with him, even on the cold days.

Thank God for Deanna because without her:

Our kids would both have dreads and false teeth by age 5 because I always forget to remind them about little things like brushing their hair and teeth. And if they resist the suggestion at all, I say, "Okay, no biggie. I'm sleepy too."

Thank God for Deanna because without her:

Our kids would believe breakfast was a synonym for "cold cereal", lunch was a synonym for "sandwich", and dinner was a synonym for "fend for yourself / ice cream's fine."

Thank God for Deanna because without her:

School would be a place you go when you wake up, whenever that is, and if you feel like it - and if you haven't been kicked out yet for tardiness and too many absences.

Thank God for Deanna because without her:

Home would be a nice place with dirt floors - not because there wasn't wood and carpet underneath the dirt, but because I don't know where the vacuum is.

Thank God for Deanna because without her:

Clean clothes would be a theory.

*Thank God for Deanna **because with her***:

Our children were born at home, breast fed, raised on life-giving healthy foods, enrolled in schools that teach to the mind, body, and spirit, treated with the respect and intelligence all children deserve, and given tireless tender loving care every day of their life.

Deanna - you are the best, most wonderful mother I could ever hope for our children to have. And you are saving them from their father's ways every single day.

Bless you!

Love, Patrick

Survival Skills

I built a fort outside with my son this morning. Fricking pain to build, but one of those things that makes you feel all the things a father hopes to feel once in a while.

You wanna feel like you're teaching your son survival skills for the event in which he's stranded on an island.

You wanna feel like you're spending quality, manly time with him.

You wanna feel like you're giving him a reason to believe his dad can build far more than his dad can actually build (which in reality is limited to being able to build nothing more than a small sandwich).

You hope to give him a memory that one day grows into family lore like, "Your grandfather once taught me build a home out of only palm trees and rope. We didn't play video games. We learned to survive on our own, no matter what! So turn that crap off and go out and build a home!"

It was my son's idea actually. The gardeners were cutting the fronds off the palm trees and hauling them away when my son said, "Wow those would make a great fort!" Now here's where I'm first satisfied with myself. I said, "Great idea son!" and I stopped the tree cutting guys from hauling them away.

Fortunately, I was the only parent home when I made this somewhat questionable decision because otherwise it would have been vetoed by higher authorities who would have surely seen it for what it was before my handiwork—a big ugly mess in the yard that threatened the grass and missed its ride to the dump (or where ever large city plants go after they die). Indeed, I threw all pragmatism to the wind and said, "Yes son, great idea!"

And then I let those things lay on the lawn for two weeks—and kill the grass.

But today... today I said, "Son, let's go build that fort!"

All you have to do to kick start any playtime with a five year old is say a sentence like "Ok, we're spies and we're stranded on an island and bad guys are looking for us so we must create a shelter," and the child takes it from there, fills in the rest of the story, creates an entire world of fantasy and needs not another thing, but for perhaps assurance that you're helping be on the lookout.

The downside is they don't *Help* to build the fort because they're too busy fighting bad guys, but hey, someone's got to fight them while you sweat your ass off trying to figure out how to turn palm fronds into a fort, which sounded insanely easy when your five year old suggested it.. But now that you're precariously balancing on top of the play set you realize the only experience you have for the task at hand is what you saw on Gilligan's Island, and it would have been far feckin easier to have let the gardeners haul these unruly palm fronds away.

When I found out I was going to be a father to a boy, I had a panic attack. Happened to me on an airplane. Suddenly I was having trouble breathing with thoughts of "What in the hell am I going to do with a boy?? I don't throw footballs. I don't know baseball. I can't dribble a basketball. I hate fishing. What am I going to do with a boy??" I really just wanted another girl. I loved being father to a girl. It was easy - no balls involved.

It took me a while, but I figured out why I was afraid of a having a boy. It was because I had no male father figure in my life - my mother raised me. I don't know what men do. And I've had a hard time seeing myself as a man because honestly, what the hell do I know about men? Somehow that translated into dreaded images of a little boy wanting to go play ball, a boy that for some reason in my mind always had snot running out of his nose. A boy I was afraid of being able to raise properly.

But it's been awesome. I don't know if I'm helping him grow into a man, but I know he's helping me learn to be more of one. We play a little ball. We wrestle. We play spies. He hates it when I play female singers that don't rock. And check it out - he found a way to show me that I can in fact save myself if I'm ever stranded on an island. Pretty cool. Pretty cool.

Thanks son.

I Bet You $100

Sitting at my makeshift desk of milk crates and a board I found in the alley, I opened the envelope that said "The Mackay Envelope Company".

A few weeks earlier I had written to #1 *New York Times* Bestselling Author, Harvey Mackay, hoping for a testimonial quote for my new book, *Major In Success*. Harvey was at the top of the publishing world with two #1 bestsellers in a row, and I was at the bottom with my first book ever.

I was 28 years young and didn't have a single warm connection to any famous or notable. Anyone. But I knew that having a testimonial quote from someone famous on your book jacket mattered a lot.

I held the envelope from Harvey's mega-million-dollar envelope company anxiously in my hand. Harvey gave out testimonial quotes like candy at Halloween it seemed because it was hard to find a newly published self-help book without a quote from him on the back cover. As I carefully opened the envelope, I felt like I was about to take a step up in the world of legitimacy.

"I'm sorry but Mr. Mackay doesn't have time to give a testimonial quote for your book," was the sentence that shattered my hopes.

Apparently he had used up all his testimonial quote time on the one hundred other books he gave one to. But really I knew it was because everyone else had a personal in. Me, from a trailer house and raised by a nurse and from a state school, and still green behind the ears, didn't have any ins.

There was only one author bigger than Harvey Mackay at the time. Tom Peters. The co-author of *In Search of Excellence*, the best-selling business book of all time. And a personal hero of mine.

Harvey Mackay was just a big name to me. But Tom Peters was the only speaker in the world that I admired. I saw him speak once and he spoke with fire, abandon, and perhaps even some spit—he was so passionate about his ideas. He wasn't a motivational speaker, he was a raving fan of what he was teaching and an expert on his subject matter who was not afraid to rant.

And he was paid well for it. He commanded close to $100,000 per engagement. Tom Peters was the man. I dreamed of having Tom Peters say that he liked my book. For me, the thought of Tom Peters liking my book was an end-all. The highest compliment possible—the last opinion I'd ever need.

But I'd just been rejected by a guy who gives everyone a quote. And Tom Peters seemed to give one to only an elite few. And to say that he's extremely in-demand would be a drastic understatement; I figured I could write to him for 10 years before I got a response. But I decided to try anyways—I truly had nothing to lose.

I figured I needed a unique approach. Something that would get Tom's attention. Tom loved audacity. Tom preached boldness. And Tom ranted about standing out or dying in a heap of those who were too scared to risk. So I thought and thought.

I got an idea.

I stapled a crisp, new $100 bill to a letter that began, "Dear Mr. Peters, I bet you $100 you're going to love my book, *Major in Success*. If you don't love it, you win and can keep the attached $100. If you do love it, I win and you send me back the $100. In either case I'd appreciate your opinion of the book."

Stapling an actual $100 bill to the letter wasn't easy on me. I was close to $25,000 in credit card debt trying to make it as a speaker, and $100 was more than I'd spend on anything outside of my career in a month. I also figured I'd probably never see the $100 bucks again. (Not because I was down on my book, but because I could see Tom being smart enough to write back and say, "Lesson in business #1, never send money unless you mean to give it away,"—which, by the way, would have impressed me.)

I addressed the envelope to his offices just an hour's drive away in Menlo Park, included a copy of my book and dropped it into the mail. Godspeed I thought.

Four days later, an envelope from the Tom Peters Group was in my mailbox. My heart rate soared. But my first guess had it as a form letter that could have said a number of things:

(1) Thank you for writing to Tom Peters. Mr. Peters receives hundreds of letters a day and unfortunately cannot reply personally to each person. Best wishes.

(2) We have received your submission and are processing it. Thank you for writing.

(3) Enclosed is the money you sent. Mr. Peters regrets not being able to accept gifts or wagers. He wishes you all the best with your book.

I put aside the other mail that had arrived and slowly opened the letter.

On the inside, I found, not a letter from the Tom Peters Group, but my own letter, the one I'd sent to Tom, complete with the attached $100 bill. Clearly, I must have gotten the "not able to accept gifts" response. But I was not done unfolding it completely. When I did, I found a sweeping line of ink drawn through the text of my letter and a hand-scrawled word at the bottom that said, "over".

I flipped the letter over, and written with a black felt-tipped pen were the following, tough-to-read words:

"Patrick Combs—You keep the $100. It is a terrific book... and I greatly admire your chutzpah. Fabulous! You can use, if you wish, the following as an endorsement: "Major in Success is as energetic as its exceptionally successful author. I wish I'd read it back in 1960 when I headed off, clueless, to college. Great Stuff!" — Tom Peters *Keep it up!

Tom's quote went on the cover of my book. There's no way it pleased any reader more than it pleased me. And the actual letter and $100 bill are framed in my office, reminding me always to take risks.

What I've Learned

You Have to Set Yourself on Fire! This has come to be a deeply meaningful principle in my life.

What I've learned is that we're all the same on the inside. We all can feel anywhere between bored and lifeless to inspired and alive. But the great freedom gifted to us by life is a moment to moment, day to day opportunity to choose to spend your time doing things that set you on fire! And by set you on fire, I mean whatever things ignite you with aliveness, passion, inspiration, love, and joy.

I love New Years because, although the opportunity to set yourself on fire is always present and renewed each moment, the start of a New Year is pregnant with symbolism and group energy for new beginnings. I love to seize this feeling every year. I love wiping my whiteboards and plans clean and gifting myself the most important question of all: "What amazing things will you take up, focus on, and indulge in that will just light you on fire?"

I am deeply aware that we motivate ourselves by

taking up joyful, exciting, and indulgent projects that feel like adventures.

And I've learned that if you don't, you perish on the inside from boredom, depression, obligation, responsibility, lack of energy, stress, and demotivation.

What I've learned is that it's a mistake of epic proportion to steer your life by your obligations and bills to pay. Instead you have to look further, farther, and grander. Fill your life with projects you love, madly truly love. When you do, your bills and obligations will be taken care of far more easily because you're on fire, *on fire for life.*

No mediocre projects. They'll kill you.

No safe dreams. They'll dull you.

No pretty good aims. They'll swamp you.

Sit yourself down with a pen and paper and dream up ambitions and adventures that on paper alone trip you into joyful fantasy. Choose adventurous ways to spend your life, things that feel like they're plugging you into a greater power source, from 20 volts to 200. Give yourself remarkable projects and infuse your life with extraordinary purpose. *Then and only then* will your dream world be built at last.

You have to set yourself on fire.

And the beautiful thing is you were born with the ability to do so on any given day.

Let your light shine by the light of your fire!

This is what I've learned.

Love, Patrick

Marlboro Man

November 14, 1993 had tremendous potential for me. It was the day of my first "lecture showcase". In the words of a talent agent who'd been working in the college market for 12 years, "A lecture showcase is fat city. You don't even have to do great—an OK performance can net you 5-10 gigs, which translates to 15 to 30 thousand dollars."

The agent's words were only boosting the high hopes I had for my big opportunity. I needed this kind of big break. I'd been working for over a year to establish myself as a speaker on the college circuit, and all of my efforts to date, which included mailings, cold-calls, and begging, had so far produced only eight dates.

The agent's words echoed in my head the entire week prior to the showcase. "You don't even have to do great—an OK performance can net you 5-10 gigs." Music to my ears, because I was officially on a roll.

I'd just done a string of gigs that had gone excellent. (Granted, it was a short string, but four lectures can count as a string. And granted they weren't in a tight row, they were actually spread out over two and a half months, but no matter, because in my book, I was definitely on a hot streak.)

It's not easy to get a lecture showcase. Once a year, you submit a lot of paperwork and a video, you pay some hefty fees, and then you wait a month to find out if you're one of the lucky four people selected from the forty or more applicants who will get to showcase.

As one of the lucky few, you get to perform a twenty-minute version of your talk in front of approximately 100 college students who are in charge of, and have money for, bringing speakers to their school. (Over one hundred prospects all in the same room at once—representing over seventy colleges.

If you don't think that's a white gold opportunity, you haven't tried to reach a college student by phone lately.)

The day prior to your showcase, you meet and greet students on the trade show floor. Since this was my first college conference, the whole experience was exceptionally exciting. Besides being incredibly optimistic, mostly I was proud. Proud because, out of the hundreds of performers represented in the exhibit hall, I was one of the few whose picture had a sign that said, "Showcasing on Saturday." And proud because of the way students were treating me.

Students saw my booth, noticed my showcasing sign, and treated me with special respect.

The day before my showcase it felt like a thousand students shook my hand and said, "I'll be at your showcase. I really look forward to seeing it. Excellent to meet you!" In no time at all, every hall I walked down in the Hilton Hotel was filled with friends and well-wishers.

I had prepared like crazy for my showcase. Scripted it word for word, rehearsed it, ran it by friends, rewrote it and re-practiced it. When Saturday morning came, I felt ready, ready, ready.

One of the most exciting things to do at these conferences is to walk the exhibit hall floor and discover and meet the people performing on the college circuit. I'd never seen anything like it before: In one row of booths you'll discover celebrities, comedians, jugglers, musicians, ventriloquists, psychics, mentalists, hypnotists, duelists, and speakers.

Of all the people I'd met at the conference, there was one person in particular who I hoped would attend my showcase: The Marlboro Man of the late 70's, Christian Haren. He was a big-time speaker on the college circuit, famous for his talks about living with AIDS.

The Marlboro Man stood out to me immediately for a number of different reasons. First of all, he was a celebrity. Secondly, he was where I wanted to be someday—a famous speaker. But most of all, he stood out to me because of the way he stood and the look in his eyes —he actually had a twinkle. Christian had confidence. He stood like a winner, walked like he was flying, and smiled like he was having the best time of his life.

I nervously introduced myself to him. He was entirely friendly. He even made a point to stop by my booth later on to see exactly what I did. He complimented my materials, gave me encouragement on my showcase, and told me to call him Christian. I was thrilled.

It came time for my showcase. I had no way of knowing if Christian was in the audience, especially since a stroke of luck quintupled my audience size. Instead of only showcasing for the hundred or so students who were in charge of lecture programming, the conference organizers decided that this year's lecturer showcase would be on "The Mainstage", in front of all 600 students in attendance.

This was a huge, lucky break.

"You don't even have to do great—an OK performance can net you 5-10 gigs," I was thinking just minutes before I began my showcase. I was so ready for my slot when I hit the stage, and I was ready to do a great showcase.

Then the unexpected happened.

Suddenly I was speaking under circumstances I'd never spoken in before. All the house lights were off and two huge and blinding spot lights were aimed on me. I couldn't see anything or anyone, and I couldn't think. I was like a deer, confused and stunned by a pair of headlights. I was stumbling over words, forgetting my script and shielding my eyes! The Mainstage turned out to be my undoing.

In a heartbeat, my big chance was gone. I got off the stage and barely knew what hit me besides immediate pain and disappointment.

Afterwards, my girlfriend would talk to me, but nobody else would. Twenty minutes on The Mainstage was all it took to go from lucky to loser, from a V.I.P. to a failure, from an overnight $20,000 to another year of hard labor.

I wished I could go home right away, but I had to suffer agonizingly through four more hours of standing in exile at my booth—on the outside chance that someone in the 600 person audience thought my talk was OK.

Turned out the answer was: nope. But even that wasn't the most painful part—it was dreading having to see Christian again. I couldn't imagine facing him, but sure enough, he came to my booth.

"Hey bud, I'm sorry that I didn't get to see your showcase, but how'd it go, did you knock 'em dead?" he asked with a big optimistic smile on his face.

"Not really," I replied, "Actually it was a nightmare."

Christian sat down and talked to me about it, and thus began lessons from the best mentor I've had as a speaker, and imprints from one of the strongest role models I've encountered in life.

"Patrick, I would have stopped everything and told the audience what was really going on inside of me. I would have said, 'Stop! Stop! I don't have it together right now because of these lights in my eyes, and here I am trying to tell you how to be successful! Someone help me!'"

Then he added, "I think it's absolutely essential to always stay honest with your audience. Only then will they trust you." It was advice I would take to heart and use to my advantage for the rest of my career.

Over the course of the next three years, our friendship grew. I learned he was a gay man who had contracted AIDS early on in the crisis. He found out he had AIDS after collapsing on a sidewalk in San Francisco. He got the news of what at the time was a sure-fire death sentence when he woke up in the hospital.

The very next week, he was the first person in America to go to a high school to talk to young people about AIDS. He wanted to put a face to the virus, he wanted to be an educator on AIDS to help kids.

I met him years years after he had spoken at that first high school. He was very humble about it—but some things he'd say would hint at him having spoken at more than quite a few schools. I think he even said the President of the United States had thanked him for his service to the Country.

I was never sure if he was exaggerating or telling it like it was. But I loved him nonetheless. He was one of the most positive, full of life, supportive friends I'd ever had.

156

Many people with AIDS say they are dying of AIDS, but Christian always said he was Living with AIDS. I saw him start writing a book for children days after he was diagnosed with a vicious and fatal disease (and I saw him work on the book every time a new doctor gave him a new diagnosis of only a few more weeks to live).

I saw him drive fifty miles to do a speech on a day doctors said he should stay hooked up to his oxygen machine. I walked, scared, into a hospital room expecting to see him dying in a light blue hospital gown, hooked up to tubes, IVs, and morphine, but instead found him sitting on the edge of his bed in blue jeans and a T-shirt. He was, in fact, hooked up to all those machines, but instead of talking about dying he was making plans for living.

"Patrick, this past week has been a living nightmare. I've been up walking around because I'm too sick to lie down," he said coughing.

I was so frightened on the inside that I didn't even catch his joke, until he said, "I've been up walking around because I'm too sick to lie down. I like that. I'm going to write that down and use it as the first line in a short story."

He then struggled across the hospital room and wrote it down, despite the fact that earlier in the day he'd just been told he had very little time left.

Once he told me his own prescription for hard times: "Every morning it's important to get up—get up and do something, even if it's just to clean your kitchen floor. You can't be a victim if you're busy and doing something for yourself. Get up. Say hello to the day. Say 'I'm here. I'm alive. I'm present.' And then go on about whatever happens."

I remember the day that yet another doctor told him

157

that he had at best only a month to live. Christian's response, and I'm certain it's what kept keeping him alive, was to go back to work on his children's book. He even finished it. And when the next doctor said, "Get your things in order", Christian said to me, "Guess it's time to rewrite my book!" *And he did.*

My showcase failure that day was among the heaviest embarrassment and pain I've suffered for my dream, but I met and made friends with Christian and that made the whole thing worth it. Christian was the good I got out of the bad. The gift I got out of the pain.

I got another showcase the following year. It went better—I got four gigs out of it. And the next year I got six. Some of us are slow to start but strong to finish.

Christian died two years later. I cried at the news. He outlived every doctor's prediction by years. As a matter of fact, when he died he was the longest living survivor of AIDS in the world.

His boyfriend called me over because he said Christian had left a few things for me. Christian had left me the manuscript he'd worked on for years, the one that he'd get out of bed for on days when he could barely walk. And he'd left me a box of newspaper clippings. In it I found hundreds of newspaper articles written about him, some with photos of him being honored by George W. Bush, the President of the United States; most documenting him speaking at hundreds of high schools to hundreds of thousands of students.

Christian must have saved thousands of lives and spread huge ripples of compassion in the world for victims of AIDS.

As you pursue your dreams, the Universe sends you mentors. Mine was The Marlboro Man.

Miss you buddy.

Donkey

The donkey's back foot was completely torn off when we found him. Bone sticking out! Flesh dangling. Blood dripping everywhere! We stumbled upon him on a path in the middle of a jungle in the Dominican Republic. And his back foot was gone!

Holy Unexpected Sightseeing!

At first we tried not to throw up.

Then we bravely froze in panic.

What the hell do we do for this donkey?! We're in the middle of a jungle. In a 3rd world country. We're just tourists.

This donkey needs a doctor... or a gun.

My son, only six, was freaking.

I'm thinking, "We've *Got* to do something. But *What*?!"

And while we're collectively trying to keep our breakfasts down, soothe ourselves and stir up some plan, the poor donkey is just standing there bleeding out.

Did he chew off his leg to get out of a trap?

Do coyotes do shit like this??

F#@! This is bad. *Really bad*.

We just wanted to hike to the cave swim. This was NOT in the brochure!

Our tour guide politely suggested we move on. We refused. She expressed genuine relief that we were the kind that wouldn't abandon the donkey.

Together we summoned a veterinarian and waited.

He arrived, looking much like the Dominican version of Indiana Jones. Perfect!

Then he took a long needle and shoved it into the raw exposed flesh. Simultaneously ensuring the donkey wouldn't feel pain and that my son will be permanently afraid of shots.

Then he took scissors—the kind with blue handles, the kind you have in your junk drawer—and cut off *a lot* of muscle. Like he was trimming the drumstick. I tried to view this as Thanksgiving at 99% of people's homes, but I couldn't. It was more disgusting. This was still attached to the live animal.

But then came the real stain on our permanent memory. He produced a hacksaw blade from his plastic shopping bag. A blade. Not a hacksaw. *A Hacksaw Blade.*

This doctor is a great Dominican hero. And improviser.

My son buried his eyes in his mother's blouse.

I forced my eyes to watch, even though they wished very much not to.

And right there in the jungle, Indiana *Veterinarian* Jones sawed off the donkey's leg bone!

How many cuts does it take to hacksaw off a donkey's leg? About 50 it turns out.

It was a blood bath.

Imagine tourists on the same trail the next day. Looking down at a significant swath of blood spattered ground, with a different tour guide that doesn't know a damn thing about our field amputation. Imagine that tour guide, trying to explain to the next family that bloody patch of trail!

Hacksawed off the donkey's leg!

In the middle of the freaking jungle.

I couldn't decide if our jungle tour should have cost less...or way, way more.

In all seriousness, it was an amazing experience for us all. When the donkey was finally bandaged, eating, and assured to be okay, our cups were overflowing with a deep feeling of joy and fulfillment.

Opportunities in life to help another living being out of suffering are great blessings. I couldn't help but notice the butterflies circling us all and landing on all our shoulders when our rescue was complete. Life is beautiful, the way it can stir us to compassion and exhilaration on any given day.

It's a girl!

A week later our three-legged donkey gave birth to a baby girl. None of us had any idea the donkey was pregnant. I guess we'll name her, Lucky.

Wannabe

19 years old was one of the most stirring years of my life. It began with a move from Oregon to San Francisco to go to college. But it really kicked off eight days after arriving, when I stumbled upon two guys playing music for a huge crowd of students in front of the Student Union.

Growing up in lumbering Oregon, I'd never seen a street performance before; the idea of one had never even dawned on me. I was gripped.

They called themselves The Square Roots, a crappy name I thought, but everything else about them was exhilarating. The more I soaked in the totality of what they were doing—they had no microphones, no amps, no speakers, no drums; just an old beat up guitar, which the tall, thin guy was strumming frenetically, and a stand-up bass, which a slightly shorter but thicker guy, was practically spanking—the more adrenaline washed through my veins.

If I am anything, I am a geek for talent. Because I'm a wannabe—in the most positive sense of the word. I wanna be talented more than a child wants toys. Talented people make human beings seem magic. But standing there in awe of The Square Roots, still a sophomore majoring in advertising, I had yet to figure out that I wanted to be talented. I only knew I wanted to keep absorbing these two rock stars.

The guy playing guitar was bobbing up and down, singing high on his toes—which were wrapped in red high-top Vans. I'd never seen red high-top Vans before. They looked daring. He was also wearing threadbare blue jeans, creased at the ankles in a tight cuff, and an old jean jacket over a white T-shirt. He was playing his guitar without any strap at all. And although he sustained it with his knee or elbow, he strummed so voraciously the guitar's pit guard looked like it had been sanded off. Sweat dripped like a leak from his messy brown hair. To maintain his ability to see, he had to shake his head like a dog shakes after exiting water. His face had a whittled but radiant look. He sung lead on most of the songs with a high, slightly scrappy voice. And when he spoke in between songs, I heard a southern-accent. His name was Jerry Wagers. He seemed like he walked right out of a Tom Petty video.

Then there was the bass player. What he wore made him look like a typical student; a sweatshirt, sneakers, and gray jeans. What wasn't typical was a giant bush of dark, curly hair that bobbed along with the beat and the gigantic instrument he was slapping away at. He pounded the bass so much in fact, that he had protected his fingers by heavily layering them with white medical tape. His sturdier, homier voice was the perfect harmony to Jerry's, and he, Tim Fuson, would grit his teeth while he played and occasionally send his station-wagon-sized instrument spinning with one mighty blow. The first time I saw him quickly spin it, I thought it maybe hadn't really happened. The second time around, I cheered.

Together they were The Beatles, The Everly Brothers, and The Violent Femmes all rolled into one. They played for three hours that day and I missed my marketing class to stay for the entire show. Right away The Square Roots shot up to number two on my all-time favorite bands list, second only to my all-time favorite, The Kinks (who occupied over 40 of the albums in my collection). But The Square Roots did have something on even The Kinks. The Square Roots were taking their music to the streets. It seemed like a brilliant concept; raw, real, and unrestricted. I was blown away.

Afterwards, I stuck around to buy one of their tapes and learn anything I could about them. I guessed them to be on a promotional tour sponsored by MTV, with a hit record climbing the charts. A worldwide tour opening for some band like R.E.M.

As I stepped up to within a few feet of them it was as if I'd stepped into a vortex that exaggerated all my faults. Suddenly I was dressed entirely uncool. My hair was way too normal. And every thought in my head was now too stupid to say. It was a feat in itself that I managed to compliment them with a very stuttery mouth. Tim seemed a bit nervous about my nervousness. Jerry seemed happy to hear my superlatives and at the same time anxious to get to the next person in line. I was just happy to have survived the encounter without tripping, and to be able to say I'd met them.

Then I hung around at that awkward distance that seems appropriate when you no longer have any real reason to stand close anymore, but you still want to hear everything. I stood there trying to discern every single word they uttered. I managed to piece together that they were actually from Berkeley, just across the bay, and would probably return within the month. I was almost confused by the reality that they could be so fantastic but live so close. But in any case, the fact that they would be back was great news to me.

Even greater was the fact that I now had their cassette, a ten-song tape titled For Sale. I rushed back to my dorm room to hear it. As it blared out of my speakers I went mad. I air-guitared. I air-bassed. I sang. I bobbed. I spun. I shook my hair—even though it wasn't long enough to shake.

As it turned out, The Square Roots were far from the celebrities I'd initially guessed them to be. They weren't even signed. What they had was a ten-song tape, a circuit of Bay Area universities that they made regularly unscheduled appearances at, and somewhat monthly Friday night shows at a little hole-in-the-wall pizza parlor in Berkeley called The Golden Boy. Golden Boy shows were the best because of the wall to wall intensity created by several hundred people crammed into a place that most felt certain "The Roots" would make as legendary as The Cavern in Liverpool.

The day, as in the unforgettable day, came nine months after I first saw them. It was October 26th and they came to play our campus. But an hour into their set it began to rain. They packed up their instruments and got ready to go home. I stood by close, as I always did, desperately wanting to be the last one they talked to, and expressed my disappointment about the rainout.

Then it happened. Jerry drawled, "Tim, why don't we finish the set in Pat's room? We could use the practice." Tim scrunched his eyebrows together for a second and said okay. If I ever win the lotto in my life, it will pale in comparison to how lucky I felt the day The Square Roots decided to play in my dorm room.

As the two rock stars were following me into the dorms, students were astonished. They'd look at The Square Roots with surprise and then they'd look at me with wonderment. Word of the happening spread like a fire through the five-story residence hall. The Square Roots were in the building following a guy who lives on the second floor. They got into my room and it was crazy. It seemed like there was just enough room for me to sit on the end of the bed, because they occupied almost all of what little space is afforded between the two single beds mounted to each wall. Playing less than two feet from my face they were Gigantic. And true to who The Square Roots were, they played no less passionately than they did on the plaza.

I invited my two closest friends into the room with me, but quickly loads of other fans started knocking on the door. Not more than six people could fit into the room, but that didn't stop the hallway from filling up. Those two made me king of the dorms for at least a good week.

But October 26th was not over yet. There was another great surprise awaiting me. As I walked Tim and Jerry to their car, for the first time not feeling geeky around them, it happened. I said, "Hey you guys are so incredible you should be signed, and playing all of San Francisco's best clubs, and in Rolling Stone, and stuff like that."

Tim replied, "You should be our manager, Pat."

And before I could fully experience the flush sensation that was racing across my body, Jerry added to the sentiment, "Yeah Pat, you should. You could be our Colonel." he said referring to 'Colonel' Parker, Elvis's manager.

I'm a big dreamer, but being their manager had never, ever crossed my mind as a possibility. I had dreamed about becoming one of their friends. I'd dreamed of joining their band (even though I couldn't play a lick of any instrument). I'd even gone so far as to fantasize that they would ask me to sub for one of them if they got sick on tour. But band manager was something I'd never thought of. Hearing their invitation was one of those moments so great that heaven might be disappointing. I said yes, and from that day forth I was one of The Square Roots.

I didn't know jack about being a band manager, but my passion for what they did outdid my insecurities about failing them. I grabbed my camera and took pictures of them. I applied myself to endlessly improve their press kit. I dared sales calls and booked them into majors clubs up and down the West Coast. I even dove into completely uncharted territory for myself and designed their next album cover. I loved doing it all. Working on their stuff made me feel like one of the most important persons in the world.

It also put me smack into the middle of San Francisco music scene, in clubs like the DNA Lounge, Paradise Lounge, Berkeley Square, Plough and Stars, DV8, and Blake's. Hanging out in these dark, swanky places made me feel cool and happening. Constantly sharing the bill with great local bands—like JellyFish, The Furlongs, and Mod-L Society, and big time acts like The Flaming Lips, The Silencers, and The Fall—fed my love of loud, passionate rock music. There's nothing in the world like the feeling of being five feet from the stage, swimming in music, marveling at musicians, and thinking, "That's my band." I was always proud, awed, and humbled.

Jerry, Tim, myself, and thousands of fans thought The Square Roots would get famous. But in the end it wouldn't be us that made it onto the pages of Rolling Stone. It would be Jelly Fish, it would be Adam—the lead singer of Mod-L Society—later fronting a band called the Counting Crows, and it would be another guy, Chris Isaak.

The Square Roots broke up over personal differences two years after I began managing them. I was prepared for the break up knowing what I knew as an insider, and it fit into that truism that all good things must end. But it closed one of the best chapters of my life.

Foolhardy

I was really in a zone at nineteen. Maybe I peaked at that age because my playfulness was very high, and my motivations were perfectly natural. I wanted to enjoy my life and I knew that the best way to do that was to just do what you thought to do, because you thought to do it.

Take the bush for example. There was a sidewalk leading back to the dorms, and there was a six-foot bush next to the sidewalk. There was no reason in the world to go over that bush—none whatsoever—the sidewalk didn't go around the bush, so it surely wasn't a short-cut. There were, however, plenty of reasons to not go over the bush, including but not limited to, it was six feet high, you would get scratched up, and all you would accomplish is a rough landing on the lawn that graced the other side. Plus you'd make a spectacle of yourself to the many students that were guaranteed to be within the line of sight. And yet that's exactly what I did a lot over the course of a semester.

I would see the bush and start running. A few feet before the wall-like shrub, I'd take a flying leap. I'd mow over the top foot of the bush every time, and keep my arms stretched out in front of me to soften the headfirst landing. I'd get up, brush off the grass and dirt, and proceed as if I'd done nothing unusual. The first time I did it was to see if I could do it. But I kept it up because it was fun.

I also gave stand-up comedy a try. For a month on Wednesday nights, I told my own "jokes" at an open mic held at a bar called Ye Old Pub and Thistle, in San Francisco. Thankfully, it took place in a dank and dim back room and the only people there were other upstarts waiting for their 10-minute turn.

Trying it made me quite nervous, but the fact that 9 out of 10 people doing it sucked, made it considerably easier. So did the fact that I never let anyone I knew know where I was. My material was the real joke, but I plugged along and each time at the mic was a rush.

I felt good on stage. I loved trying to make my audience laugh. It culminated in me doing a 30 minute "set" in a Saturday night variety show put on by fellow dormies. The campus cantina was packed wall to wall, and I knew everyone. A part of me begged to disappear right before going on stage but I wanted my chance to see what I could do. It went all right—mostly because I was cracking myself up—and I actually got a lot of laughs. At least that's how I gauged it until the next guy did his act.

The next guy was Rob. He had students unable to breathe for 60-minutes straight. I'm sure anybody there that night still remembers his imitation of Elvis on a Fish hook. Picture Elvis being pulled up by the mouth with a fishhook and that's what this little guy made himself look like. Stupid but very funny. Rob later made it big on *Saturday Night Live* and in movies. His full name is Rob Schneider.

That was the last night I did any stand-up. I was looking for something different but I didn't know what.

Once, on a Thursday afternoon the week before

Spring Finals, I dressed like a homeless clown and went down to the crowded shopping district of Union Square to rant about the day's headlines. I did it because of a guy named Stoney Burke. Stoney, a thin little guy that looked like Ross Perot's younger brother, would often come to San Francisco State costumed in high-water plaid pants, clown-sized leather shoes, thrift-shop shirts and a balding head. Dressed like a fool he would plop a ratty briefcase down dead center of the crowded student plaza, take a newspaper out and start riffing off the headlines.

He always started off slow and picked up speed over the course of a couple hours—despite being mostly ignored by the hundreds of students just wanting to enjoy the afternoon. And he was a spitter, like Daffy Duck. He ranted with so much conviction saliva flew yards from his mouth. But so did razor smart, and often-hilarious wit.

"Hmmm, let's see what's in the news. McDonald's tries out McRibs. I bet they do, the Multi-zillion, commie, Pinko, Nazi, capitalist, bourgeois bastards who worship the Quarter Pound weakling, Ray Kroc, every day after they close the drive-thru. Oh Mr. Kroc, please tell us the story again of how you cleared billions and billions of acres of rainforest to create the Big Mac... And the bedtime story about the monkey who gets tortured to make the fries taste better..! Or the one about your ties to the CIA..! That's right, McDonald's has ties to the CIA—what do you think of that?! Well since none of you want to discuss it, let's see what else is in the news."

Although the topic kept changing, Stoney seemed to have a purpose that was constant. He was continually inviting students to participate in the topic at hand. It was as if he imagined he could rally an impromptu town

171

hall meeting. But nobody was ever game, except for the occasional misguided frat guy who would try to defend Ronald Reagan, Stoney's favorite target.

Since they could never match wits with Stoney, they would either quickly back down, or threaten to beat him up. But as soon as they started threatening to smash his face in, it quickly turned into three stooges-like hilarity. Little Stoney, big-eared and spectacled, running in circles from a beefy frat boy. Stoney would still be yelling insults and citing his first amendment rights. When it truly got too close for his comfort, because some of them really wanted to beat the shit out of him, Stoney would grab another, larger pair of glasses out of his jacket pocket and spew, "You wouldn't hit a 97-pound weakling with a pair of glasses, would you?!"

Most of the students who witnessed Stoney had zero interest in his theatrics, which led me to believe that most of them were lacking the gene for excitability. I thought he was a genius, and the bravest son-of-a-bitch I'd ever seen. I not only wanted to participate in his impromptu town hall, I wanted to try leading one myself. So I did just that.

On a sunny afternoon in April, I went down to Union Square, the heart of San Francisco's shopping district, and tried to act like Stoney. I went out there in plaid thrift shop store pants, newly acquired for the occasion, along with a worn-out briefcase that contained the newspaper. I even have big ears. But that's where the similarities ended. It was so difficult to do what Stoney did.

Actually I was scared from the moment I woke up that morning.

The fear got more and more real as I rode the MUNI train downtown. It peaked the moment I picked my bustling street corner and opened the San Francisco Chronicle to begin.

First of all, looking through the paper, I realized I had no clue what to rant about. Where Stoney was politically intelligent, I was an imbecile. And I wasn't angry about anything. I had no agenda. How was I supposed to get other people riled up when I couldn't find a single article that pissed me off? Secondly, I was scared shitless to look up from the paper and begin yelling. I grew up in a town where if you were going to say anything to a passing stranger, you'd say, "Hi, have a nice day." Now I was challenging myself to look at well dressed, random passerby and spew conspiracy theory and spit. I tried it.

I kept looking up and engineering short bursts—very short—of inoffensive, unprovocative, unintelligent drivel, followed by a reading of an entire story out loud in a pathetic attempt to stall. People, nice people, would hear it and just keep walking. I know they noticed me because they'd have to step around me a bit. But very few looked and only one guy stopped. He offered me 35 cents because he thought I was selling papers. We were both embarrassed by the mistake. At first, people ignoring me made me feel like a jackass. But about thirty minutes into it I began to feel relaxed and alive. I liked that I was taking a chance, doing something different, and that I had beaten my fear, whether people noticed or not. The only problem left was that it was Stoney's gig, not mine. I was missing a gene for ranting. So at the end of an hour, I returned to my dorms and threw the plaid pants away.

Looking back on my sophomore year in college, I can see that I was working overtime to become somebody—somebody that stood out. My urges to perform, the same urges that would later propel me to my career as a speaker, and then later as a comedic performer, were showing. But at the time I couldn't see myself as an artist. I saw myself as a straight man, a normal, and a regular. I still thought I was going to be in advertising. I guess the absence of artists and performers around when I was growing up made me unable to see what I obviously really wanted to be. But I was following my bliss and my bliss was moving me forward.

My daughter is learning sign language. She's teaching it to her little brother—3 years old—also. Excitedly he told his friend this morning, "Yes I am learning sign language! Wanna hear it?"

Sorry Starbucks

WARNING: This story is graphic, not to be read during any eating activities, perhaps to be avoided all together, strictly for shits and giggles but a decent cautionary tale. Read at your own risk.

I like to start my days with healthy smoothies. And in some way, when I do, I feel like it makes me just a little bit sexier from a good food, good mood energy glow. I do smoothies with fruit, kale, coconut juice, nuts, hemp, and such types of natural goodness. But today my wife Deanna made me a smoothie of her own concoction. As she handed it to me I failed to remember that about every smoothie she makes is an attempt to make an EVEN healthier smoothie.

She handed me a pale green colored smoothie that looked like something the dog threw up. But I never care about the color of a healthy smoothie and I liked the flavor of it, drinking it while I drove my kids to school. But then I find something on my tongue that I can only describe as feeling like a small piece of skin. As a matter of fact, that's the perfect description of what I found in my smoothie; something that felt like a small piece of skin, and it's sitting on my tongue and I'm a little reluctant to swallow it.

So I text Deanna, "What are the little skin pieces in the smoothie?"

She says "they're chia seeds and that my text made her gag."

My text made her gag? How about "I'm sorry."?

Truth be told though, I just block the bad texture out and continue drinking the smoothie because my mind is a hundred other places anyway (all of them random and unimportant to be certain).

Anyway, I get to Starbucks where I settle in to do some writing with my son in tow, and then within minutes, I very much have to go to the bathroom because I feel the pretty urgent need to sit on the toilet. And so I do. And it's like the scene in Dumb and Dumber, I full on have diarrhea—the explosive kind.

Not how I saw my morning going. Not in keeping with how I like to utilize any Starbuck's bathroom. Diarrhea is the instant humbler. All vision of self-grandeur flushed down the old toilet. So much for sexier.

I try walking out looking like maybe all I did in there was wash my hands and freshen up. And I figure I lost so much weight on that toilet that I'm certainly done with bowel movements for the day. Maybe two days.

But I'll be damned not 30 minutes later my son is trying to tell me that for Halloween he wants to go as the video game character, Steve, in Minecraft, which only requires he wear a box on his head which is great really, and I can't wait to see him walking around proudly as a block head from a video game because he's going to look so cute, and a box for a head is within my range of costume making. But suddenly I can't hear him to the end of his costume description because I feel the mass exodus coming on again!

This time I'm practically running to the Starbucks

bathroom—hello toilet bowl, so soon we meet again! Apparently my body had plenty left in deep storage, because again, much is evacuated.

I leave the bathroom many more pounds lighter, again trying to walk out looking like maybe all I did in there is shine my shoes, but surely someone in that Starbucks saw me practically running to the bathroom, so it's doubtful I fooled them. And hey, can someone tell me why on God's green Earth every bathroom doesn't have spray fresheners for the love of all things important?!

Anyway, I've heard of healthy green juices being capable of causing diarrhea but this smoothie Deanna made me really went above and beyond the call of duty. So I text Deanna and it goes like this:

Me: "Your smoothie gave me diarrhea! Like you added a pint of cod liver oil! What kind of wicked concoction did you make me?? What did you put in it?!"

Deanna: "Omg I'm dying."

Me: "Your smoothies are evil!"

Deanna: "I spiked it with enzymes."

Me: "Well those enzymes are now in the Starbucks toilet. TWICE.

And I RAN the 2nd time!"

Deanna: "Omg I'm laughing my ass off."

Me: "What are enzymes anyway?"

Deanna: "They help you digest your food. I may have put too many in today."

Me: "You think?... If by digest you mean liquify, mission accomplished."

Usually eating healthy is much more fun, I'm a vegan 18 years now, not a single piece of meat, no fish, no chicken, no milk, no cheese, etc and I love it. Vegan is great for my body, good for my soul, awesome for my energy, got me straight A's on my blood work this month, and it's very good for making a personal positive contribution to a clean water, and clean air and a sustainable planet for all living things—but today it gave me diarrhea, thank you very much.

Beware the enzymes. Starbucks, I'm so sorry.

Raymond

This weekend I met a man while walking with my kids. He was sitting on a park bench. You could never tell by looking at him, but his driver's license confirmed that he was 93 years old—exactly twice my age. He'd lived through basically the last 100 years.

Raymond lets you in emotionally in a way that creates friendship fast. For half an hour he told us powerful and poignant stories about segregation, WWII, and Martin Luther King Jr. He had experienced severe racism for most of his life.

Hearing stories about his life prompted me to ask him two questions I've pondered many times. I looked into his eyes, which because of age looked like pools of mercury.

"Raymond, if when you die God greets you with two questions, what would your answers be? First: Did you enjoy your life?"

Raymond smiled and said, "Very much! The good and the bad. Every second of it."

It was wonderful to hear him affirm the goodness of life, apparently acknowledging its perfection.

I asked my second question: "If you lived again

would you do anything different? Any regrets Raymond?"

He went deeply silent and then this oh so elegant and strong man began to have tears streaming down his face. Tears I didn't see coming and that made me feel concerned. Finally he spoke.

"Yes, I'd have been kinder to some people who I knew along my way... My grandfather used to say 'There's no strangers. We're all from the same race. We're not from the fish race. We're not from the animal race. We're all from the human race. No one is a stranger. And the most important thing is to be kind to everyone you meet.'"

Sometimes it seems like life gives you an opportunity to act on what you were just taught.

Shortly after meeting Raymond, we drove by a woman and her daughter with a cardboard sign asking for money for food, for her three daughters. And something about this woman looked especially vulnerable - like poverty was a new crisis in her life, not a habit.

It turns out she only spoke Italian, which I do not. But we took her and her daughter into the nearby grocery store and we bought them a cart full of groceries. The woman thanked us as best she could in every aisle, but our true reward was a tremendously wonderful feeling in our hearts, for having met Raymond just in time to remember the importance of kindness.

The Soul of the World

The Soul of the World can talk to us. And it does. At least it sure seems like it does.

The other night I was out and about with my good friend Brian. Brian was contemplating a bold move to San Diego to pursue a whole new career, but was very uncertain and full of fears about doing it. As we walked San Diego's downtown, I spoke about my belief that when we're following our heart the world helps us along with signs, omens, synchronicities, and coincidences. An idea I was first exposed to in the book. *The Alchemist* by Paulo Coelho. Coelho refers to it as the Unspoken Language of the World's Soul; a secret language of hints that help guide you to your destiny.

I've experienced so many coincidences that it hardly seems reasonable to call them all coincidences. For instance, I write in my journal about something I want to come true, and then the next day I often "happen" to meet someone who can help my dream come true. Or I'm talking to someone about one of my ambitions and a really motivational song comes on the radio.

I remember one particular day when I was scared

to quit being a well-paid marketing agent and to try becoming a full-time, on-my-own, professional speaker. I was at my desk pondering the leap into what seemed like risky financial waters when I finally said to myself, very loud and clear, "That's it. I will not do any more marketing for someone else. I vow to go for being a speaker—and I trust the universe will support me." Rrrriiing, Rrrriiing, went the phone. I picked it up and *Yes!* It was a totally unexpected sale that put $700 in my pocket. It was as if the Universe rang my phone—and it left me in awe because even 911 doesn't respond that fast.

Anyhow, Brian and I were headed for the Horton Plaza Mall and I was going on and on, ranting that I also think the Universe only speaks to you when you're following your dream and listening to your heart. If you're clinging to a life raft of security, or paddling around in shallow and comfortable waters, the Universe is silent. No hints. No clues. Why should it?

Brian's taking this all in, having an open mind. But he's also giving me that look like, "Patrick, maybe you've been in California too long." (We grew up together in Oregon). I understood his uncertainty. I was doing a crappy job explaining the phenomena I believe in so much. It's hard to come up with enough convincing coincidences. And, what seemed like a direct communication from God yesterday, seems today, like, well, just a coincidence.

Anyhow, within seconds after pitching Brian on reading *The Alchemist*—a fable about a shepherd who journeys across the Sahara to follow his dream—we turn a corner and practically walk right into a large shop window decorated with a photo of a camel and rider crossing the desert. I exclaimed, "That's what I'm talking about, Brian! Is it coincidence that the shop window is decorated to illustrate our conversation, or is it a sign that what we're talking about is true? I think the Universe can even use shop windows to communicate with us!"

Brian said, "Hmm," while his head movement signaled yes and no.

We took literally five more steps and we saw the next sign. There in a shop, emblazoned across the wall for decoration, were the words, "Be bold and mighty forces will come to your aid. —Basil King". I was now freaking; these "coincidences" made me exuberant. Brian was now nodding his head more yes than no.

We continued on to our destination, the Successories Store, so I could purchase some gifts to give away at my talks. I introduced myself to the sales associate and pointed out that my book *Major in Success* was stocked on their shelf. I hoped he would ask me what it was about so that I could get him excited about recommending it. He did something much more unexpected. He totally ignored that I was the author and launched into a story about how Damon Wayans got his start in comedy.

According to this man, Damon tried stand-up comedy on a dare and was told by the comedy club owner, "You've got it, kid. You should move to Hollywood." Damon went home and told his parents the exciting news. They were not excited about the idea of him leaving everything behind to pursue talent they didn't see him possessing. The point of the story, the man told us, was that often, the ones closest to us don't see our gifts or talents. We have to believe in ourselves.

When we walked out of Successories Brian turned to me and said, "It's strange that that guy just launched into that story, but I'm not surprised. I think I'm beginning to understand the Unspoken Language."

We got in our car and turned on the radio. The song

playing was Get What You Give by the New Radicals. Brian and I looked at each other smiling when we heard the singer say, "This whole damn world can fall apart. You'll be ok. Follow your heart!"

A month later Brian moved to San Diego to follow his dream.

The Viking

There I was this morning standing naked in my bathroom without a towel anywhere near me to be found because I'd put everything in the wash the night before, including every towel. And my path to the dryer where the towels are is blocked by guests. And it's freezing.

So I'm just standing there dripping wet in my birthday suit trying to figure out how to dry off, and refusing to use a T-shirt because they absorb NOTHING and are only slightly better than taking wax paper to yourself after a shower, they just move the water around on your skin and feel insulting.

I don't even have an itty bitty wash rag which I've used plenty of times before to dry off with, so for the first time I got NOTHIN to dry off with and it's really too cold to drip dry and I refuse to put on clothes while I'm wet.

So I'm wondering if I *have* to use a T-Shirt, when I look down and see it—the bathroom rug. And it's calling to me because it happens to be super shaggy and highly absorbent.

But I know that no self-respecting person would dry off with a bath mat because doing so would be disgusting behavior. After all it sits right on the floor, right near the toilet, catching everything that falls or drips; the dirt from your feet, the hair that falls out of my head, and, well, everything, as I'm sure you can imagine. But also, no one's around to know if I do use it, so...

I picked up my shaggy blue rug off the floor and start rubbing it across my chest and then my arms. Slowly at first but then the more I drag the heavy unruly super shaggy thick rug across my naked parts the more I get a surprising feeling—the feeling like I'm a Viking; a manly, tough, real life Viking drying off with bear skin or dragon fur or what not.

And I like it.

By the time I'm onto wiping my back and my privates, all caution is gone, I'm doing it like I've been using large thick bath rugs to dry off with my whole life, and I start thinking maybe THIS should be my towel always instead of the thin girly towels I wasted my money on.

How was your morning?

Christmas Lights

Sometimes I wonder about decorating for Christmas. I once fell off the roof onto my head putting the damn lights up... But that's a story for another day.

More specifically, every year as I'm hauling boxes of ornaments and lights and reindeers and penguins and trains out of the garage, I think to myself, "Why am I doing this??"

At the start of my "decorating day", when I'm trying to get myself motivated to walk the l-o-n-g walk to the garage to get all the boxes of holiday stuff (our garage is like a mile away), I wonder, "Am I really going to hang Christmas lights on the outside of the house, just to take them down in 3 weeks? Am I really going to spend the better part of a day on a ladder, up and down with a staple gun, when in fact, we're almost always in the house after dark and don't see the lights much anyway?"

And then I question if I'm really going to do the *Long* walk back to the garage to pull out the Polar Express Train, and then crawl *In and Around* the tree, assembling the track just so the train weaves its way through the Christmas presents?

What is all this *Temporary* decorating for?

I'd rather be watching football. I'd rather be running errands. I'd rather be cleaning my office to tell you the truth.

Perhaps once a year, we succumb to the societal, cultural expectation that we too participate in the decorating madness. I think we do. But shouldn't we say, "I refuse," and stop the insanity? We can't be sheep who just buy lights and Santas and elves and trains just because we're supposed to. This is actually the stuff I think while I'm doing the *Long* walk to the garage. Yes, I'm *That* guy on a bad day. *And I Can Be That Lazy.* The garage, if you must know, is a 2 minute walk... Okay, I'm exaggerating, it's only a 1 minute walk... Or more realistically 30 seconds, okay 15 seconds I suppose... at a good clip—but still...

I admit, at the beginning of the decorating process, every year, I just can't think a good reason to unpack and put up the lighted penguins, lawn reindeers, the lights that go on the bushes, the icicles on the windows.

But then...

But then I get into the process and it becomes a project and as with all projects, I get swept up in doing the job and time passes efficiently. It could even be said I'm feeling productive.

And *Then...* many hours later...

The lights are hung on the eves and twinkling, the penguins are placed by the door, the reindeer are on the lawn, and the train is ready to chug around the track.

And Then...

My son sees the Penguins and squeals with excitement, pointing and stumbling in front of them as only a delighted 1 year old swept up in wonder can. And my heart grows a size. My daughter rushes to sit at the controls of the train to engineer it around the tree and through the presents for the 10th year in a row. And my heart doubles again. The icicle lights twinkle through our windows, warming the smiles on both of my children's faces and also please my wife. And suddenly, the biggest light hung in the room now *is in my heart*.

And I think to myself, "Ah yes, again I almost forgot, we decorate for love and for joy."

But do be careful when you're putting those lights on the roof. Your head will thank you.

I Love My Kids

Once you've had kids, there's something deep in your soul that knows how deeply it matters that you love them. As if that is your real mission in life.

I am painfully aware of all that I don't do for my kids, of the mistakes I make, of all the fatherly aspirations I hold in my heart but I simply never reach.

When I fail to reach a career aspiration sometimes it hurts, but it doesn't break my heart.

I have one high hope now that I always carry with me—I hope when my children are grown they feel they had a good father. And if I'm bloody honest, I have to admit I hope they miss me when I die. And why would I wish such an awful selfish thing?

I guess because in my silly little mind it's the way I imagine I'd know I mattered to them. And I deeply want to matter to my kids. I guess because if I matter to them then I must have been good to them.

So how do you matter to your kids? It's the hardest job I know and a job description that every parent is familiar with.

I try and wake them with a hug or a kiss. Love them every day with words and hugs and deeds. Reflect back their greatness with compliments. Give them real attention with undivided presence. Spice up their life with adventure.

I try to encourage their dreams. Show them enormous respect for their individuality. Show them I've got their back. Let them see me being a human being with strengths and weaknesses. Role model for them a person trying to make the most of life. Teach them a little. And I try and tuck them in at night.

And lord how I fail in so many ways that honestly hurt my heart.

Having children revealed to me two beliefs I didn't know I possessed. One: that every child deserves a parent, someone who will be their constant in life through thick and thin. And two: that every child deserves more love than most of us adults can give even on our best days.

I thank God for my children and I hope to God I can live up all they deserve from me.

I am certain of one thing: if you can love your kids well, then you will be rich beyond measure in the ways that can't be counted, but that really count.

Pursuing Your Dream

How it *Feels*. Good, bad, and ugly.

First of all, it ain't easy. Don't let any one kid you. Pursuing your BIG dreamiest dream will shake you down and show you all your weaknesses. So we who pursue our dreams risk more than money—we risk feeling like failures. And along the way, we often do feel like failures.

Secondly, it's as exhilarating as great sex. *Word*. Because as you pursue it you find that you are a far greater person than you ever knew. Your dream will make you feel like a rock star just often enough to help you put up with how damn hard it can be.

Thirdly, it's scary. Not always, but often enough to make you want to curl up in a ball, stay in bed or pick up an application for Starbucks. You have to overcome a voice inside yourself that says shit like, "What the hell am I thinking?! I'm not good enough. I suck."

Fourth, it's magical. The minute you really commit to achieving your dream you set into motion a series of small (sometimes large) miracles that come to your rescue. Amazing synchronicities become your way of life. Like the entire Universe is conspiring to help you.

This week alone, my dream has made me like a failure, like a rock star, afraid, exhilarated, alone, and like an invisible guiding hand is coming to my rescue. It's a roller coaster ride for damn sure. Perhaps it's not for everyone. There are easier ways to go.

But for some of us—me and perhaps YOU—we'd have it no other way. Because pursuing our dreams is what makes us *Feel Alive*, what makes us *Feel Rich* and what gives us the feeling that our life has *Purpose*.

Are you one of us?

Is it time for you to pursue your real dream?

Love, Patrick

Twenty five years ago, the VP of one of the largest clothing companies on Earth asked me my dreams. I told him I wanted to speak and write.

He, of enormous stature, said, "I used to think of writing fiction but then you learn you have to be practical because there are bills to pay and a family to support. What else would you like to do?"

I thought to myself, "Quit working here and get started."

Add Friend

I met Aaron just about a year ago. We met because of work, had a nice conversation over coffee, then we agreed to something really unusual. Something guys basically never do.

I said, "Hey Aaron, how about we have coffee and just talk about life once a week, maybe for a year? We won't try and figure out some way to work together. We'll just talk about life. I think it could be rewarding."

I was looking to have more real, authentic, non-Facebook, non-work, friendship in my life. Being a full-time father, a husband and a careerist—well that keeps you pretty busy. Time to just hang out with a friend, what's that?

But more than being busy, the reason for my suggestion ran much deeper.

I know a lot of guys whose every friendship is really just an extension of their work. Their guy friends are co-workers, colleagues, associates, or collaborators. Their friendships happen through work meetings, or mastermind meet-ups. Everyone is viewed as a "friend" but it's really just "work" that bonds them together. Their circle of friends might as well be called "professional association meet ups". This is a real guy-thing.

I started noticing this five years back. I left a business I was involved with where I had "friends" all over the world. But the minute we didn't have work in common, all those friendships dried up overnight.

Nowadays, I seek to fill my life with friends who don't value me through the lense of work. Life's too short. And I'm clear that friendship isn't real if it only happens through FB and the occasional meet up—where you hug your buddy and say, "How's it going? What's up with your work?"

Aaron said yes to my suggestion and our unusual guy-friendship experiment over coffees began.

Could we sustain it?

Would it fizzle quickly without the usual guy-bonding agent of work?

We kept making the time. Kept having coffees. And kept work talk to a minimum. About 3 months into it, it started to fizzle. We went a month without a coffee meet up, a single text or call.

It was failing, because there was no work to make the guy-bonding thing easy.

Work has urgency. Work has bottom lines. Work is a strong bonding agent for guy "friendship", like an epoxy. But non-work based conversations, was proving about as bonding as Elmer's-glue. Nice but easily dissolvable.

Add to it that we were trying to bond over coffee, not alcohol. Yeah, we were way out on a limb here.

But we picked back up in May and continued on. And then a funny thing started to occur... Life kept happening to each of us, ups and downs, rewards and pains, and we kept sharing the experiences over coffees.

Somedays, I'd walk into the coffeehouse happy and share why. Somedays I'd walk in down and be real about it. Other days, it'd be coffee to mostly hear about Aaron's tremendous personal breakthrough. And then of course there were days where something was weighing heavy on his mind.

Funny, I barely knew anything about the day to day workings of Aaron's incredible career, but I came to know the inner workings of his day to day feelings.

One day—just about 1 year into this friendship, developed 95% over coffee conversation—as Aaron saw me approaching, I was so completely out of sorts, he took one look at me and said, "Buddy, what's the matter? Talk to me."

6 hours later, he'd help me turn around a really shitty day.

So work never became the glue between us. Or alcohol. Or adrenaline sports.

We've never done a work project together. We've never done any J.V. of any kind. We've never invested a dime on one another's endeavors. I don't believe the guy's ever seen me speak or stopped by my website.

Instead, it was the consistent sharing of our journey as two people just trying to navigate this crazy thing called life that created a true friendship, an actual friendship, one that has zip to do with Facebook.

The whole thing taught me something about friendship.

True friendship isn't easily forged. Nowadays the word "friend" is as simple as an "Accept Request" button, and often just as hollow.

Nowadays, too many men fill their lives with "friends" who are in actuality, just colleagues, and I feel bad for those who confuse the two. They are far from the same thing.

An actual friendship takes a ton of conversations to develop. But is worth every dollar you may spend for coffees.

Extraordinary Love

It was September 2002 and I had this little ball of anger in my abdomen. I called it my little ball of shit. I could just feel it sitting there left of my stomach, it was fist-sized and pissed off. Granted, it was strange having a shitty, little ball of anger in my body. It was a first.

There was no denying it was there. I'd notice myself on-edge throughout my days and immediately recognize the source of my problems was this exactly tennis-ball-sized angry spot near my gut that just wanted to punch someone.

I'd say to my wife, "I don't know what's going on but I have this little ball of anger, of shit, right here in my body - it won't go away—and it's been there about a month now."

"That's weird," she'd reply.

It was weird, but I'm a matter of fact guy and the fact was that it was there. I didn't know why. I didn't know how. But I knew it was so. On the outside, things seemed good in my life. Sure, life stressors, relationship imperfections, work challenges, but still nothing out of the ordinary that would seemingly explain this strange unusual phenomena spoiling my mood all day.

So I began to think that this unusual problem needed an unusual solution; I began to think I needed to try an "energy healer" for the first time in my life.

Okay, I lied. I had tried an energy healer once before. It was years ago in San Francisco and the woman's "healing" session consisted of massage and loud, continuous, vulgar belching. Short belches and long belches. "I am releasing negative energy from your body and it makes me belch," she explained between disgusting sounds.

Who am I to say if she was or wasn't releasing negative energy from my body, but I can assure you she was adding more negative energy into my body than could ever be released in an hour. I swore off energy massages and got into therapy.

Anyhow, I picked my second energy healer out of a free newspaper in San Diego. Her name was Marsha and her ad said "Massage & Energetic Healing." Her photo was in the ad as well, she was a brunette in her late 40s. Her smile made me feel like there's no way she could be a belcher. She seemed to have a genuine friendliness in her face.

Now obviously the hard thing about "energy healing" right upfront is that you can't feel "energy". It's like saying, "I'm going to heal you magically using undetectable, invisible rays from the Andromeda galaxy. It's painless, as a matter of fact, you won't feel or see a thing." So it's a real "take it on faith" proposition.

And then there's the price. If you can heal me without touching me, well then you are a wizard my friend, and I'd expect to pay a Wizard in gold. So I'm prepared to hear that Marsha costs $300-$500. I'm hoping for $300.

I called Marsha and found out her price. $55 for an hour! Surely no real wizard charges such a pittance. I hesitated to set the appointment. Maybe if she'd said, "$100". But $55—it practically doomed me to more belching. None the less, I wanted my little ball of shit gone. So I risked it.

When I walked in the door Marsha greeted me. Her almost-black hair was pulled back tight against her head. Her skin was lightly freckled, apparently from age. And her eyes looked serious, almost skeptical. She didn't seem to care if I felt welcome, which surprised me. She began with questions.

"What kind of work do you want today?"

"Some massage and I'm hoping for some energetic work too. I want to find a person who while massaging me can pick up on what else I might need, you know, and energetically heal me." I never felt as ridiculously new age as I did after saying that.

"That's exactly what I do. Is there any particular issue or injury that brought you here?"

"Well yes. Sort of. I had a very angry September. And even though the issue is resolved, I can't get rid of this ball of anger and shit right here," I said putting a tight fist to the spot on my abdomen right below my rib cage.

"That's very intuitive of you. That's exactly where anger gets stuck in the body. Good, that guides me a lot."

She told me to undress and lie face down under the sheets of the massage table. She gave me a minute to do so, returned, put on relaxing music, and gave me a firm, professional massage for 30 minutes. And then she spoke, "Are you ready to begin with the hands-on-healing work?"

"Sure," I replied.

She pulled the sheet up to my neck and placed her hands over my abdomen. Within seconds I felt heat coming from her hands warming my belly.

I was a little confused. How was I feeling the warmth of her hands since they were above the sheet and not even touching me? Had they heated up from the friction of giving a massage? But I knew logically that her hands were hotter than friction could explain. So I asked.

"Did you rub something like Icy-Hot on your hands?" I thought she might say, "I dipped them in a natural, homeopathic, ancient, Indian lotion that aids in healing."

Instead she said, "No. That's just our Chi interacting."

"I can't believe how hot it is. What's Chi?"

"It's the energy that powers the body. Pretty cool huh."

Pretty Twilight Zone, I thought to myself.

Soon after, the same heat began rising in my stomach just underneath her hand.

"Now I'm feeling the heat in my body under your hand!"

"You might feel energy shifts elsewhere in your body too."

I didn't. But I noticed that I thought her hand was not on the right spot. I could feel this exact place just a couple of inches lower that needed attention. So I told her and she adjusted her hand. Then it happened. My entire abdomen lit up with heat. No longer just underneath her hand. Like the size of a heating pad. It was incredibly vivid.

My stomach began gurgling. The ball of anger began melting.

"I'm feeling all this heat! I'm totally feeling this! I can't believe it."

"You're multi-sensory," she exclaimed.

"What's that mean?" I asked completely bewildered at everything that was happening.

"You can feel beyond the five senses. You can feel your energetic body too. How old are you?"

"Thirty-six."

"Really? Oh, I thought you were much younger. More and more young people are multi-sensory and you look younger."

"I can totally feel this. I've never felt a healing working before. Can you tell me what's going on?"

"It's actually pretty straightforward. Someone figured out how to work with the bio-energetic body and created Shen Therapy."

I was surprised she could talk and work, but we were talking a lot because I couldn't believe I could feel so much heat moving in my body. Then I noticed my body talking to me again, this time requesting her hands up by my heart. I told Marsha.

"Yes, I was just headed there," she replied.

She put her hands over my heart and I didn't feel much. She'd not placed her hands exactly where I felt my body's need, but her hands were close to the spot so I waited.

But hardly anything was happening so I decided not to wait. Without asking I adjusted her hands to the left a few inches. Five seconds tops went by and then boom, a tidal wave of red heat rose up in my knees and legs and raced toward my chest—from my knees!

"Oh my God! I'm really feeling that in my knees and legs and all over my chest!!" I exclaimed.

Marsha kept her hands in place while I burst out talking about what I couldn't believe I was feeling.

"Oh my God, now I'm feel all this joy," I said almost laughing from the happiness that was washing over my body.

"That's good. That's your heart energy," she said almost too calmly.

"Unbelievable!! I can't believe this! Does everyone feel this with you?"

"Shen is very powerful. Your body seems to take to it especially well though. Often people don't feel this much for a number of sessions."

Then completely unexpectedly, the joy became a wave of sorrow. Enough to put a lump in my throat. I thought maybe something was going wrong.

"Why am I feeling sorrow now?" I asked even though I assumed she would have absolutely no answer.

"Because we're opening your heart chakra, and joy and sorrow go together. That's good. That's what we want."

She kept her hands in place for many long minutes until the heat and feelings subsided.

The ball of anger that I'd felt jamming my system for a month, was gone. When I sat up, I took a deep look at the woman that had just transformed my entire view of life. I saw confidence and peace in her face. The next thing I noticed was a tall white wall poster with seven pastel colored, flower-like symbols. It was stunningly beautiful.

"What's that poster of?" I said feeling completely peaceful.

"The Chakras. The yellow lotus flower is the one that we worked on today for your anger. The green is your heart Chakra."

For the first time in my life I knew that I really did have an energetic body and that Chakras were real, so I had to have the same poster. She told me the shop down the street where I could get it. Before heading to the store, I scheduled another appointment and paid her. She said I owed her $55. I wrote her a check for $100.

I walked out of Marsha's place feeling renewed physically, happy, sort of tingly, clear, and most definitely healed. I was also starving—with a capital S—something I hadn't been for a month. That night I didn't sleep well because my body was ringing with energy.

Second Session.

Three days later I returned to Marsha's office. "This time we won't talk. Last time you were so excited and wanted to talk about it so much, it was okay. But today let's work in silence," she said.

We also agreed to skip the massage part so I laid on the table fully clothed.

The session went very differently. I felt almost nothing except when she put her hands over my throat. Her hands over my throat produced a lot of heat. Outside of that, I felt so little I assumed the session was a bit of a bust.

Perhaps there was nothing else for me to heal. At the session's end, Marsha asked me what I'd experienced. I told her about the only thing—besides my throat—that I had to report: imagery that would come and go. Some image would pop into my mind, a few seconds later I knew the meaning of it, but as soon as I did, it was gone and I couldn't remember a thing about it.

I thought Marsha would shrug it off. She said, "That's exactly what we want. We're clearing a lot of old stuff. As it releases, it momentarily passes through your mind. But when it's gone, it's gone and that's why you can't remember it."

I liked the idea of old stuff being cleared.

As I wrote Marsha a check, this time for $75, she said that she'd been instructed by the Master Teachers that were guiding her, to expand and stretch my energy field during this session.

"You should feel pretty good the next week from the work we did here today," she said. I asked her if I should do a third session. "Your energy body looks very good. Your heart chakra is a little wobbly, we could work on that if you like."

I made an appointment to come back. I requested Monday at 2 p.m. Marsha said okay, but then requested I come at 10:00 a.m. "10:00 a.m. is a peak time for our bio-energy."

I left feeling extraordinarily vibrant in my body. It made me remember that my body used to feel this vibrant back in my teens. The feeling would last for days. It was also an amazingly clear feeling.

Third Session

The following Monday I was back in Marsha's small, spiritually decorated healing room. The previous day had brought a lot of upset. I felt tired. I knew my energy wasn't flowing. And because I felt like I'd gone backwards since I last saw her, I felt guilty. She asked me if there was anything in particular that I wanted to work on.

"My heart chakra. Last time, you said it was a little wobbly."

I climbed up onto the massage table. Marsha put

her hands over me. I wasn't feeling much, experiencing any imagery, or having any intuitions as to where my body needed work.

The magic of the first two sessions was gone and Marsha's hands reflected what I felt was happening, they kept searching for a better position, never settling, never finding the right place. The session was going nowhere.

I was disappointed. I'd been told once before by a psychic that my heart energy was wobbly, and I wanted to get to the bottom of it. I wanted it healed. So I began praying.

I pleaded for help from God and any spirit guides I might have. "Please, heal my heart. Please bless me with healing." But soon, in a dimmed room with relaxing music playing softly in the background, my prayer dissolved into spacing out. I don't know how long I spaced out, but I know it was suddenly interrupted by a vision. The most vivid vision I've ever had. Like it was really happening:

A girl, probably 12 or 13 years old, opened a door to let me out of a pitch-black space. I must have been in a shed or an outhouse. She was standing under a blue sky, in the backyard of a farmhouse. I could see a cornfield behind her, edging the un-mowed grass.

I had time to gaze at the beautiful girl. Olive skin. Defined cheek bones. One beauty mark. Brown hair in braids stuck close to her head. Staring at her holding the door open for me, I began wondering who she was, and what this was about. Is she someone from my past? Is she an angel? Why this yard and shed? There were no answers. Just a girl I felt like knowing and thanking— and she was holding the door open for me. Then the vision ended.

Then just as suddenly, I felt the first thing I'd felt the entire session: heat travel down my spine, top to bottom. Marsha had one hand on the top of my head and the other at the base of my spine.

I began to think about my mother and how she became suicidal when I was sixteen. Having no dad, and with my brother having already moved out, it was tough.

I don't get emotional about it anymore. I worked all that out in therapy during my twenties. But staring up at the ceiling, I realized that the one thing I couldn't get from my depressed mom was kindness and comfort when I felt stressed. It dawned on me that that was what I was looking for from women ever since. Made logical sense.

Marsha moved her hands to my waist. They shuffled around for position. Then she put one hand on my abdomen and one on my left hip.

Without warning, I was hit with a wave of true sorrow and I burst into crying. No, not burst—exploded. Then my belly erupted into a swirling red heat and my crying expanded into a hard, convulsive cry that wouldn't stop.

Then heat, unlike any heat I'd ever experienced, filled my entire chest. It was rising and it was golden. Perhaps it didn't even feel like heat, but rather like pure energy. I was being worked over by two separate energies that divided my torso into halves.

Marsha said loudly, "This is what Shen's all about! Just let it all go. Try and keep your breathing grounded." My crying was out of my control. It was like water rushing through a dynamited dam. I couldn't fathom where this lake-load of sadness had been stored.

Marsha's hand moved as if they were holding a crumbling wall together. My hands jumped in to help cover spots I intuitively knew needed it. "Good, you're assisting in your own healing," she said.

I cried for 20 to 30 minutes!

When my crying finally subsided I felt totally up-ended. I was damp and empty of whatever energy enables a person to move. Completely spent. I laid on the massage table without moving for what would be another half-hour.

While lying there, I realized that the girl in the vision had opened the door to my healing. I wondered if Marsha had seen her as well. I bet that she had. I also knew that I'd been crying about the hardship I suffered because of my Mom's severe depression.

"Do you know who the girl was?" I asked.

"I didn't see any girl, but I saw your Mother."

Not once, ever, had Marsha and I said a word about my mom. The confirmation hit me like another wall of water. And crying broke out again. This time a conscious reaction to how good it felt to have had the buried sorrow specifically acknowledged and addressed.

I told Marsha of my history with my Mom. She said, "Yeah, well I definitely saw her right here in your body." She pointed to the right side of my chest.

"Your mom also gave you great gifts." Marsha said.

I took her comment as a pleasantry.

"Marsha, what just happened?"

She explained that when I'd arrived, energetically my body was cut in half. "For the first hour I worked and worked to reconnect you but was getting nowhere. I was practically yelling for assistance from the Master Teachers. And they were all here for this one she said. Buddha, Maitria, Jesus, Krishna, Muhammad, and finally they gave you a golden shaft of light down your spine."

"I felt it! I felt that light down my spine," I exclaimed!

"It was a great gift. And when your body recon-
nected we were able to work. I brought in Theta energy
which most people can't handle but I thought it might
really help with you," she said.

"What's Theta?"

"A higher frequency of energy. Usually we spend
our waking hours in Alpha and small amounts of time
in Beta, but Theta and Delta we only experience in sleep.
Anyway, it really worked for you."

"How do you know when different Master Teachers
are assisting?" I had so many questions.

"Oh, the longer you do it the more you get to know
how they feel, or sound or talk. One will have a real sense
of humor, another just a particular feeling."

I had more questions for Marsha. For one thing, I
wondered about the humming-bird like vibration I was
now feeling in my outstretched arms.

"This vibration I'm feeling in my arms isn't like the
tingle you get from hyperventilating. What is it?" I asked
marveling at the sensation.

"Well, technically, it's energy from the Sun. It's very
good for you so just enjoy it," she replied.

The vibration soon spread to my chest and legs.
While it was doing so, Marsha told me more. "When you
got your breakthrough and started crying, a huge wave
of Joy exploded through the room. That's very, very
good," she said. "And your guides gave you the gift of a
total cellular-level memory clearing."

"A total cellular cleaning?" I asked. "What's that
and how do you know?"

"I saw it," she said almost surprised that I would ask
such an obvious question. "It's like a golden-laser beam
that goes over every inch of your body and refreshes
each cell with a clean wash. It's a very great gift. Don't

be surprised if the world never looks quite the same to you again."

Laying there, I knew nothing in my life ever would be the same because of what I'd just experienced. Not only had I released something huge, but I'd experienced the mystical.

Now I knew that energy bodies, chakras, spirit guides and Master Teachers—were true. And I would be able to live from that truth without reservation.

I still couldn't move an inch—I was steam rolled by spirituality and I could barely believe what had just happened. I asked Marsha if all her clients get a major healing like this.

"Some take longer than others, especially war veterans who often take more than 30 sessions to get their breakthrough. Three sessions is rare. Like I said, you responded really well and even participated in your own healing. You could probably do this work with training. But more often it takes seven to twelve sessions," she explained. "But you were courageous today."

"Why do you say that?" I asked.

"Because it takes courage to come in and say you want to heal your heart. And these healings don't take place unless you really want it."

I remembered how sincere my prayers were when the healing was going nowhere and felt good about myself.

I wanted to know everything this woman saw and knew. But as I slowly lifted myself off the table and realized our session had gone an hour and a half over the scheduled time, I thought to just ask one more question.

"Why did you say my Mom gave me great gifts?" At first I'd assumed it was just a courtesy remark, but now I wanted to check.

Marsha again looked as if I'd asked an obvious question. "Because I was told. I don't know why I'm told certain things during the healing but I am."

I'd long ago concluded that my gifts for speaking and inspiring had been the other side of the coin of my mom's depression, which often took her to depths of pain so dark that she would attempt to take her life and often speak of wanting to kill herself.

Marsha had more to say about it. "It takes an extraordinary amount of love between two people to agree to play the roles you and your mother have played for each other during this lifetime. And apparently you followed through and used the experience to develop the talents you wanted."

Her words touched me deeply. I'd never thought of my relationship with my mother like that before. Her role as a depressed mother helping me develop my depths as an uplifting personality.

Beautiful.

I asked Marsha if I needed to return for another session. She laughed as she pulled on a sweatshirt that surprised me because of a Billabong surfer's logo. She said, "No, you're done. You are definitely done. You may want to come in for a tune up six months from now. But I don't need to see you again anytime soon."

"Marsha, what were you before you were a healer?" I asked.

She smiled somewhat sheepishly. "A social worker." I connected the diplomas on the wall with her statement. "Believe me, I didn't want to be a healer. But once you get the calling you can't deny it. I was like, okay, I'll do some massage, but I'm never running an ad that says 'Energetic Healer.' That was 15 years ago."

This time I wrote her a check for $500—a true Wizard's worth.

On the drive home down California's I-5, I felt more alive, fantastic, loving, and perfect than ever before. In my car I was spontaneously yelling, "God Bless! God Bless! God Bless! Thank you!! Thaaaaank you!!!"

Patrick tells these stories and more at:

http://YouTube.com/PatrickCombs
http://SoundCloud.com/Patrick_Combs

Acknowledgements

My deep, sincere thanks to my friends Roland, Vauna Byrd, and Cathy Baker who guided the book through editing and publishing with both talent and selfless love. I'd also like to thank all my Facebook readers and friends who over the years have been my true source of encouragement to keep writing. Thank you to my wife Deanna for being the star of many of my stories and of my life. Thank you to my children, Alyssa and Will, for being truly the two best ongoing stories I've ever known and loved. Thank you to my brother Mike for being such a great brother and being an original influence in my storytelling. Thank you to my friend Ken Goldstein for being a source of great encouragement. Thank you to my mother, whom I'm sure is still watching over me, for telling me long ago to take risks in life and to do what I love. And most of all, I'd like to thank the mysterious force behind all of Life for everything that I am and for every story I've ever had to tell.

Invite Patrick to Entertain and Inspire at Your Next Event

"Master Storyteller" "Impeccable Comic Timing" "Star Power" "Uplifting" "Inspiring" "Jaw-Droppingly Funny" "Hilarious" "Standing Ovation"

Patrick is a world-class storyteller, a masterful entertainer, and a renowned inspirational speaker. He has been the invited guest speaker and humorous entertainer of more than 1500 organizations and theatres around the world.

"This guy's got Star Power."—Variety magazine

Invite Patrick to entertain and inspire at your next event and he will wow your audience with masterfully told stories and his infectious and uplifting good spirits. His unique and unforgettable performance mesmerizes his listeners and leaves everyone feeling amazed, happy and renewed.

"Combs has his storytelling down to an art."—Time Out NY.

His skills as a humorous storyteller have taken him on a rocket ride that resulted in him being discovered by HBO and invited to perform in the three most prestigious comedy festivals in the world, (US Comedy Arts Festival, Just for Laughs, Edinburgh Fringe Festival) and Off-Broadway in New York. His first show, MAN 1, BANK 0, was an international, smash-hit and presented more than 400 times in theatres around the globe.

In the world of inspirational speaking he is included in the Motivational Speakers Hall of Fame and his clients include Visa, Homewood, American Heart Association, Optum360, MBNA, Citibank, First USA, Vital, Shell, McGladrey, Aventis, Motorola, Boeing, State Farm, Ariix, Stanford and NYU.

Patrick has appeared on *Good Morning America, The Late Show, ABC Nightly News, NBC Nightly News, The View, CNBC, BBC,* and *NPR.* His story has been featured in more than 500 international media outlets, including *The New York Times, the Wall Street Journal, USA Today, The San Jose Mercury* and *The San Francisco Chronicle* in which he was the cover story for delivering a stranger's baby on the sidewalk, while on his way to work.

WHEN YOU ARE BURSTING is his 4th book. His other books are MAJOR IN SUCCESS, GEARING UP FOR A GREAT LIFE, and MAN 1, BANK 0.

For booking information visit:
http://patrickcombs.com

DIVE INTO THIS SNEAK PEAK OF

MAN 1 BANK 0

PATRICK COMBS

An Epic True Story. Read by More Than 1 Million.

He put a $95,000 phony, junk-mail check into the ATM
as a joke. It cashed! Then things got *really* crazy...

You May Already
Be a Winner

Ralph Waldo Emerson boldly stated, "Don't be too timid and squeamish about your actions. All life is an experiment." In May of 1995, I suddenly found myself smack in the middle of a very unusual "life experiment." I deposited a phony check into my ATM as a joke. It came as junk mail, pushing a get-rich-quick scheme. To my absolute astonishment, it cashed. Thus began the wildest adventure I've ever been on in my life.

Present Balance

As I step up to use the outdoor ATM, and there's a blond-haired young man wearing a knitted Rastafarian hat panhandling for change. His cardboard sign makes me laugh: "*If you lived HERE you'd be homeless by now.*" I give him a dollar in change. He's a regular by First Interstate's Haight-Ashbury branch.

After fifteen minutes waiting in line for the ATM, it's finally my turn. As I step up to get some cash, a little window on the panel slides from green to red. It now says "closed."

What? No. This is not perfect service, I think to myself.

I glance over at the other ATM working to my left. To use it I would have to cut into the line, or start over again on the wait. This is not perfect service. This is a mistake. I round the corner and walk up First Interstate's dirty steps.

I get the cute red-headed teller. She's friendly.

"Hi, how may I help you?"

"Hi. Uhm, listen. I waited in line for the ATM, and then right when it was my turn, it closed," I say.

"Oh, I'm sorry about that. It's being refreshed."

"Well, might I have $5 for the inconvenience of having to come in the bank—you know—because of the $5 Perfect Service Guarantee?"

A man $45,000 in debt cannot be blamed for asking.

"Well, you're still able to do your banking, sir. I *can* help you."

"I know, but the wasted time in line and having to come into the bank—definitely not *perfect* service. Know what I mean?"

She's smiling. She thinks it's funny.

"Oh ...okay, sir. I see what you're saying. Here's your $5."

And with that, she hands me a crisp five-spot.

I will marry this teller, grow old with this bank, and always hunt for ATMs that are closed.

I ask her for my bank balance, which, as I struggle to make ends meet, consistently bounces between a couple of thousand in the black and several thousand in the red.

"Twelve years with the bank, Mr. Combs. You must have opened your account when you were nine."

Flirting with me. I didn't see that coming.

"Actually I was sixteen—At nine I was amassing my great fortune."

"I understand. Here's your balance, Mr. Combs," she says, smiling while sliding me a slip of paper that says on it, "$43.12"

"My other account is offshore."

"I understand. Have a good day, Mr. Combs."

Shit, and with $7,000 worth of bills sitting on my desk and only three checks coming in the next three months of summer, I'm going to have to open another credit card.

$95,093.35 Enclosed

On the way into my home, I grab the mail from the black mailbox that hangs on the iron gate that encloses the stairs. One is a check for $2,250 from a college where I did one of my motivational speeches. Another is also a check from a college, this one for $1,750. This is a banner day! But, alas, three more bills are in the stack. Two from credit card companies—each carrying a minimum balance due of more than $300.

And then I see it. In the stack of mail there is a gray envelope with a small cellophane window which displays a check inside made out to my name. On the envelope it says, "95,093.35 *enclosed*."

I don't believe it for a second, but nonetheless I will take the bait and open it. I will relish the opportunity to see a check for all that money made out to my name, even if it's not real. A man must have dreams. And a man must look *just in case* he *actually* won something. Perhaps a contest that he'd forgotten he entered. Perhaps a random drawing that has made him rich overnight. So you open the envelope to look, and to dream even if for just a brief moment. But you tear the envelope knowing there is no real hope. Knowing Ed McMahon loves the tease.

This letter is not from Ed McMahon. This letter is from a schemer named Mr. Mitch Klass, who offers to be my "new business partner" and who tells me the $95,093.35 check inside, made payable to me, might as well be real.

"*Patrick Combs, I expected to hear from you by now. Take a close look at the check above. It's just a sample of the money you could be receiving soon.*"

Everything about the check looks *ultra*-real.

Bank account and routing numbers.

Signature.

Office of Treasurer.

Date.

Check number.

For "**the sum of $95,093dols35cts**."

Payable to my name.

With the words "NOT NEGOTIABLE FOR CASH" typed in the top right-hand corner.

A red headline says, "*We'll teach Patrick Combs how to make $95,093.35 in just three weeks! We took in that amount in just three weeks. Other mail boxes have also made HUNDREDS OF THOUSANDS OF DOLLARS!! In fact, your mail box, at 326 Carl Street, could be soon be STUFFED FULL OF CHECKS in varying amounts and FREE MERCHANDISE!! Now I've written to you several times before about an exciting new MONEY MAKING OPPORTUNITY. The one that said, 95,093.35 IN JUST THREE WEEKS!! The same one that was featured on TV! And frankly I'm surprised I haven't heard from you yet. Patrick, I know what you must be thinking, 'Is this for real?' Let me assure you,* *it is very real. There is a MULTI-MILLION DOLLAR market just waiting for you!!"*

Shut up—you had me at hello—I'll deposit it already. But seriously, the letter goes on and on for eight pages of continual references to BIG MONEY in ALL CAPS followed by at least half a dozen exclamation points. It's highly likely that Mr. Mitch Klass is the exclamation point's biggest fan.

Getting phony, come-on checks isn't new to me. They seem to come almost weekly these days. But all of them are not worth the paper they're printed on because of the words *"Not negotiable."* A funny choice of words, this "Not negotiable." Could it mean to say that you can't try and negotiate with your bank to get more money for the check—that the value of the check is set firmly at $95,093.35—take it or leave it?

Maybe it was that thought that got me thinking about how delightful it would be to deposit this fake check as a joke. Maybe it was just the thought that such a large deposit into *my* minuscule bank account is a joke in and of itself. At twenty-eight years old, my account balance is so low I often have to question what justifies me not just using a piggy bank. Five-year-olds usually have more money than me. And that's precisely why it seemed so damn funny to deposit a fake check for almost $100,000 into my bank account. It would be an unmistakably ridiculous deposit that for sure could only result in a teller's laughter. So off to do it I went.

Prepare Your Deposit

First, it is an odd sort of pleasure to key in a $95,093.35 deposit. I'm usually done keying in my deposit amount after three digits, but today that was only half way. So this is how the rich and famous feel at their ATMs. Their banking amounts are significant. Ironically, this is the first day my deposit amount doesn't feel like a joke. But I have not forgotten that my check isn't real, and so when it's time to endorse it, I do so without a signature, with only and simply a hand-drawn *smiley face*. I am proud of my mark; it screams good humor.

Then my attention goes to the scrolling mouth of the machine that is wanting to eat my check. I have a flash of doubt that the ATM will accept my fake check. Surely magnetic ink is being accounted for. I picture the ATM will choke on my check and spit it back like a vending machine rejecting an old dollar. Perhaps a light will then flash on the screen that says, "Bullshit!"

As the mouth of the ATM is scrolling and hungering, I have a moment of hesitation. Maybe the bank won't think it is funny. Yes, of course the bank will think it's funny. It's like depositing Monopoly money, and if that's not banker humor, nothing is. A teller will chuckle at the sight of the absurd fake check and then call me on Monday morning to say, "Mr. Combs, the check you deposited on Friday wasn't real..."

"Can you make an exception, just this once?" I'll ask.

And together we will share a laugh, a small bonding.

My fingers release their hold on the check, and the ATM eats it up like a cat licking cream.

I grab my deposit receipt and, for the first time ever, I walk away from my bank laughing. I have done good.

Reality Check

Admittedly, I remember nothing else from Friday, May 19, 1995, the day of my prank deposit. There must have been nothing else to remember about it. My journal has nothing noted, my calendar nothing marked, so it must have been a completely ordinary day. The kind that almost doesn't matter in the big picture of your life. The kind of day that blurs together with all the other days when you wake up, shower for twenty minutes, work, eat—or forget to eat because of working—briefly talk to a friend over the phone, hope for sex, struggle with a relationship, daydream about your dreams, use the bathroom—and check the mail.

Since I'd also received credit card bills in the mail that day, it's a safe bet that I spent some time that day managing my debt. I manage $5,000 of monthly minimum credit card payments on a shoestring budget and keep interest rates down by moving $45,000 of debt around like a game of musical chairs. Whenever a new low, three-month introductory rate is offered by a different card, I move the money, or call and play credit card companies off one another in order to get better rates.

The only other thing I know about that day is that I worked at my home office desk on the speaking and writing profession I'd been working hard to establish for myself the past three years. The entrepreneurial endeavor was the reason that I had $45,000 of credit card debt. That, and perhaps the fact that the book I'd just had published for college students was being returned by bookstores *en masse*. Nonetheless, my career was hitting stride. I was speaking at colleges around the country about thirty times a year. My topic? Success, of course.